Once Married to Satan

My Life of Hell

TAMARA DAILY

Fulton Books, Inc.
Meadville, PA

Published by Fulton Books 2021

ISBN 978-1-64952-980-0 (paperback)
ISBN 978-1-63710-016-5 (hardcover)
ISBN 978-1-64952-981-7 (digital)

Printed in the United States of America

This is the story of my life as I lived over fifteen years in pure hell, and the abuse I endured, as a lot of women do. And that's why I dedicate this book to all the women out there who are going or have gone through the hell I did. And sadly, there are many women who can relate. I dedicate this to my baby boy, Daniel Lee, who horrifically died at age four, in 1991. My heart is still not whole. His death is like a recurring nightmare I can't wake up from. A house fire took my baby when he was four years, twelve days, and six hours old. And last but not least, I dedicate this to my daughter and four other sons. I also dedicate this to my husband, Marvin, who has encouraged me to tell my story.

Preface

I have changed the names of most people, unless they are deceased or I have permission to use their names. I am writing my story in hopes it will help other abused women and so one day, my children will finally know the truth. They do not know all I went through. Only what Jesse drilled into their heads, and of course, it was all my fault. He made me out to be the villain, a whore, and the one who broke up the family. My kids are so screwed up from Jesse, I didn't want to add to it. And it didn't matter what I would have said; they always believed what he told them. When the kids got older, I did tell my oldest son, Amos, a few things when he asked. He was in therapy at the time, but he's never really heard the entire story; the true story. I want to give hope to women, as much as I went through, and I endured a lot! I have, for the most part, overcome this. Each year gets easier, so, ladies, there is a silver lining. You will never forget it, but you can move on and lead a happy life. And there are some good men out there, as I have been blessed with my current husband. There is a calm after the storm. I want to say, ladies, if a man hits you once, it will only escalate, and you are in for a miserable life. Get out while you can. You don't deserve to be treated badly, to live in fear, be controlled, afraid to go to sleep at night, afraid to speak your mind, be used as a punching bag, or get awakened by being choked.

I was punched like a man would punch another man. I spent many sleepless nights in great fear. I spent many nights hiding in a bush or under something, waiting for him to pass out or for daylight. And that was if I got a chance to run and get outside. There is nothing more terrifying than having to hide and fear for your life. To pray you live another night. Hiding in a bush all night, behind or under something, praying he doesn't find you. When I wasn't being punched, Jesse would stomp me. He would kick me so Hard. Many times, he'd kick me as hard as he could in my butt or low back. Most of the time, it would lift me off the ground. That finally resulted in my having to have a level three back fusion in 2014. The doctors said I was a text book example of an L3 back fusion they rarely do. I have pins, plates, screws, and rods in my lower back. When my back finally went out, I was bent in half, and it was horribly painful. My husband took me to a chiropractor to see if he could help. He took X-rays and said, "Man, your ass is crooked. Were you in a car wreck?" I said, "No, my first husband." He laughed and said, "I am not laughing at you. It's funny how many times I have heard that. You'd be surprised." I said it's not funny, and no, I would not be surprised.

I have been awakened by him choking me, punching, and even peeing on me. He never waited for anything. When he wanted sex, he was going to get it. He never waited more than a few days after my giving birth to a child. It didn't matter that I had stitches. And even the doctors telling him he needed to wait six weeks. I think that only made him want it more. That was also the reason I had two babies in one year. It was all about Jesse. His feelings, his wants, and his needs were all that mattered. He was very selfish and heartless. Just plain evil. All abusers only care about and think of themselves. I have started writing this so many times. The pain is still very much real. For many years now, I have tried so hard to forget that part of my life. It's very hard to do when you have children involved, and the monster you are trying to forget has really left his mark on them. My first husband is so much like John Bobbit. He is his twin. He brainwashed my children and taught them many bad ways. No respect for their mother, women, or anyone. And he taught them that hitting a woman is okay. Or it seems not to be so wrong in their eyes. It kills me to hear of my boys abusing a woman. It shows me they do not care and how their dad treated me and all the abuse was fine, or that's how it seems anyway. I have tried to write it without using nasty language. But there is no other way to portray my story since that is who Jesse was and is. Although I pretty much bleep the words, I still want to apologize in advance for the language.

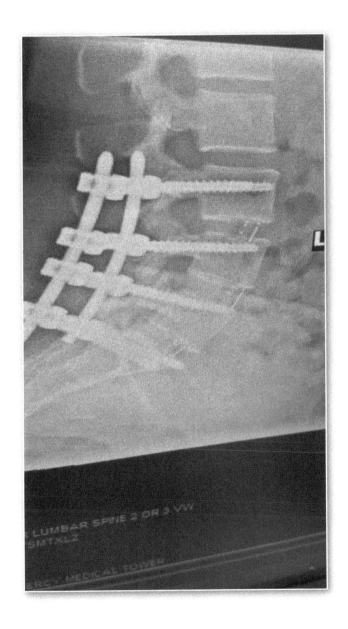

Introduction

I often wonder what goes through the mind of an abuser. How do they think? How can anyone abuse another person, much less a person they say they truly love? Well, it's evil! They are just plain evil! How can a man beat a woman he claims to love and takes an oath to spend the rest of his life with, an oath to love, honor, cherish, and protect her? Well, after spending fifteen-long years with such a person, fifteen long years in hell, I can tell you, it's Satan! So there's no statute for rape or murder. Well, what about abuse? A woman never gets over being abused. It affects her the rest of her life. Some women are stronger and can cope with it better. Some women can't cope, and there are some who just hide it well. But the bottom line is you never get over it, you never forget it, and it stays with you a lifetime. We should make them pay. If nothing else, make them pay where it hurts— their pocketbook. They should have to pay some form of restitution to the women they have hurt. If they are on Social Security or SSI, it should be taken out of their check each month. If they don't have any money left, who freaking cares! No, it doesn't even begin to make up for the pain and suffering I endured, or my children, but it would help a lot of women and children who have been so affected by the abuse they cannot hold a steady job or they are on medication just to cope with life.

I am so very thankful that the good Lord made me as strong as he did and has been there with me through it all. The Lord has helped me overcome a lot. He has saved my life on many occasions. I am able to function and have a happy life with my current husband. I thank the Lord for giving me a good man. I was beginning to think there weren't any out there. Women never forget the things men do and say to them. It sticks with them a lifetime. It is often replayed over and over in her mind. As you will read, I had such bad luck all around. I still ask myself why. And what. What did I do that was so wrong to have all this happen to me? Was I being punished the rest of my life for choosing the wrong guy? Why have I been so cursed? It sure as hell feels like it. I have always thought of myself as a pretty good person. I always tried to live right to the best of my control. And I always tried to be nice to everyone and think of others. I tried to help others as much as I could.

I hated the evil things Jesse done and the way he treated others. I hated the drinking and drugs, but it was out of my control. I didn't have control of my own life. He controlled my life totally. I was told what to say, when to say it, how to act, how to feel, how to dress, who I could talk to, and even as much as how I could love and interact with my own children. He hated to see me hug and baby our kids, especially my boys. He would tell them they were little p——— for loving up on me. We would sneak around to hug and say *I love you* most of the time. He made my kids feel like they were doing something wrong if they hugged me or cuddled with me. So he made them feel like they were doing something wrong for showing their love for me, but it was okay to talk back to me, cuss me, blackmail, and even grope me.

My Hero

Lorena Bobbit is my hero! I remember hearing about her and John Bobbit at the time it happened, but I didn't know all the details until I seen her movie just here recently. At that time, it was a very dark place in my life, dealing with abuse and the hell I was going through. I do remember saying at the time she should have used a butter knife and put it in a garbage disposal where they couldn't have sewn it back on. Lorena told my story. As I watched the movie, I was watching my life. The only difference is my life with my Satan started in 1985, and it wasn't until 2000 that I finally got away from him. But I still had to deal with him. We had six children, five living. I was younger than Lorena when my hell started. I felt so bad for her, having to have an abortion.

My Satan was Jesse. He was John Bobbit's twin, I swear, but Jesse never told me to have an abortion. Kids were his ticket to not working. He acted identical to John Bobbit! Everything John done to Lorena, Jesse done to me. I can't count the times he came in drunk. I tried to act like I was asleep, but it didn't matter to him. He'd start punching or choking me, cursing me to wake up and do my wifely duty. He'd tear my clothes off and have his way with me and it was okay. We were married, and he owned me. It makes me so sick to hear of what these evil creeps do to women. So kudos to you, Lorena Gally Bobbit! She found the courage to do to her Satan what me and so many other women only thought and fantasized about.

I wasn't only degraded by Jesse; I was degraded and done very wrong by doctors, lawyers, the judge and the court system. Where was my justice! I was happy for Lorena, getting to somewhat tell

11

her story in court, a chance I never got. And although she was found not guilty, I still feel John somehow won. He didn't have to pay for anything he had done to her, and he came out making a lot of money in porn. And I am sure his abuse didn't stop at Lorena. If truth be known, he abused many other women. Just like in my situation, Jesse never had to pay or be held accountable for anything he had done to me or any woman. And he abused every other woman he was with after me. My name is Tamara. I'm from a town in Arkansas, and like Lorena Bobbit, I once was married to Satan.

The Abuser

Most abusers come from an abusive family. They watched their father beat their mother or siblings. And a great majority of women who find themselves in an abusive relationship came from a similar situation where they witnessed their mother in an abusive relationship. And sadly, that was my situation. I watched my mother get beat from a husband and a boyfriend. I remember one time, Mom's boyfriend came over real early in the morning. We were awakened by her screaming. Bob had her in our kitchen. He had poured hot coffee on her and ripped her blouse off. He was screaming and cussing her, telling her to tell him she screwed some guy. He was a real strong man. He hit the top of her dresser so hard it split in two. She was yelling at him to leave. But he wasn't going anywhere. I jumped in front of her and told him not to touch my momma again. He said, "Oh look, you have to have your little girl take up for you. Tell her what a s—— you are, tell her you screwed him, tell her, you f—— b——."

I said, "Don't you touch my momma. You need to go." But he kept getting madder and madder. My sister and brother came in, and Bob gave us some money to go to the store. I didn't want to leave, but my sister said we need to go. Bob told us to go and that it was okay, he wouldn't hurt her anymore. On the way back, two blocks from the house, I heard Mom screaming. I took off running, and when I got to the house, he had Mom in the bathroom, pulling her hair out and shoving her head in the toilet. I started screaming at him to leave and told him the police were on their way. "Leave now!" Finally, he got up and left. What is it with these idiots pulling your hair out?

That seems to be a well-known move among abusers, along with the punching, biting, and choking. Little sissies.

So we would end up moving in Bob's house. He wanted Mom close at hand. I can't count the times he abused her. He kept his bedroom door locked at all times, even when he and Mom were in there. His house had one phone jack. He had like a sixty-foot phone cord so the phone could reach any room in the upstairs part of the house. I always got real nervous when I seen the phone cord under his bedroom door. I pretty much knew he was going to beat Mom. He started taking the phone in there after one incident when he was beating Mom and I threatened to call the police. Like many times, I remember hearing Mom scream, and Bob was screaming at her. I could then tell he was choking her. As I put my ear up to the door, I could hear her gasping for air. As I usually done, I started yelling at him to leave her alone or I would go call the police. But he wasn't too concerned since he had the phone in the bedroom. So I started beating and kicking the door. He kept screaming at me to go away and stop. But I told him, "No. You leave my momma alone."

He kept saying, "You better get the f—— away from the door." But I wasn't going to until he opened the door so I could see Mom was okay. At this point, I couldn't hear her at all. But he had choked her so much she was just trying to catch her breath. I started beating harder. He finally opened the door and chased me down in the basement. The stairs to the basement were right by his bedroom door. My bedroom was in the basement. I was really scared at this point. I knew I had really pushed his button. He was naked and running after me so I knew he was pissed. So I ran out of the basement door and out in the yard. I was yelling at him that I was going to go call the police. I remember this was early in the morning, and I didn't go back to the house until after dark. I wanted to make sure he had left for work. He owned a bar, and Mom worked for him. This was a regular occurrence with him locking Mom in his room and beating her. But I tried my hardest to protect her. I only wish I could have been more brave and stood up to Jesse. But it's totally different when it's actually happening to you. I was never so relieved when Mom finally got away from him for good.

Some people would say, "You should have learned from it," but unfortunately, it doesn't work that way. In Jesse's case, he had several men in his family who were very abusive. Not only to women but children. One cousin was sent to prison for abusing an infant and the mother of the child. He has spent most of his life in and out of prison. Getting out and abusing women every time. Doing drugs and robbing people. I believe he doesn't want to stay out. He gets out long enough to get plenty of drugs to take back with him and get his jollies off abusing women. An uncle of Jesse abused women all his life until one woman finally had enough of his abuse and killed him. Jesse told me years later how his uncle Butch would get women, have his way with them, make them do god-awful things, and one time he slit one's throat and threw her out in front of an emergency room door. Jesse always acted like he hated his uncle Butch but I think he acted just like him. And he peed on his grave one night. Just sick!

Men are great at manipulating women to the point of controlling them and using fear as their number one tool. They believe they own you. You are their property, and so whatever they do to you is okay because you belong to them. They will make you believe you have done wrong, not them. Nobody will ever believe you, and no one will ever want you because they've ruined you for all other men, especially if you have children together. They wear you down, make you feel ashamed and unworthy. You may say no to sex or something, but it does not matter. They own you when you get married. Jesse always said it was his right and it was my duty. It was okay if he forced himself on me because he was the man. I didn't have a say in anything. He had papers on me. I know years of abuse is what caused the many autoimmune diseases, anxiety, and stress I have to this day. I still get anxious and nervous if I am gone very long, if I talk to someone very long, especially a man. I know I don't have to worry about it anymore, but it's hard to get over. Even after being out of that situation over eighteen years now. It affects you the rest of your life.

My heart goes out to any woman who has been abused or is in an abusive relationship. I just want to go rescue them. I feel for them. I wish I could help all abused women and children. It took over ten years for me to stop saying "I'm sorry" for anything and everything. Every day for fifteen years or more was so stressful I didn't know what not to be stressed felt like. Nor how to live without fear daily. When there are children involved, it is so much harder to escape. What is has done to my children kills me every day. With each year that passes, I can see their dad in them, mainly my boys. I've always prayed that after my boys watched their father physically and verbally abused me, and many girlfriends after me, they would turn out totally different from him. Jesse has taught them not only how to treat women badly, but also drugs, alcohol, deception, manipulation, and disrespect. And like their father, nothing is ever their fault. I pray every day that my boys will soon wake up and realize they do not want to be like Jesse. Recognize that everything he done was wrong, was evil, and not want to live hurting the people they love. Thinking they have to manipulate and deceive people to get love. Or deceive themselves. Jesse allowed them to drink and do drugs very young. He done it with them. And he had them get drugs for him.

My Life of Hell

As with all abusive men, the first several months were good. Jesse would do things for me and tell me how he was going to take care of me the rest of my life. I would never have to worry about anything. Slowly, the hitting started. The first time, he slapped me so hard my head felt like it was on fire. I heard ringing and could smell and taste blood. I was totally in shock. I remember we were driving down the road. He was drinking, of course. We were listening to the radio, and his brother was in the back seat. I remember his brother said something funny, and I laughed. As I was looking out the window, he says, "B, was that funny. How's?" as he hit me. Later, he would apologize and say he loved me and it was the whisky that made him do it. He will never hit me again. He had a filthy mouth. Every other word was f——, among many others. For many years I thought my name was ignorant b——, or the one I really hate is the C-word. He had no respect whatsoever. He didn't care who was around. He'd throw those words out like it was normal. That's where my boys get it.

And he didn't care who was around when he hit me. I know we had to have had some good times, some happy times, but for the life of me, I cannot recall any, other than the birth of each of my children. I used to strongly believe that once you had a child with a man, you were to stay with him until death do you part. Jesse knew that and used that as well. After several years, my belief changed. It's not a good life for your children when there is abuse in the family. I was not allowed to talk or even smile at another man without being accused of wanting to sleep with them. I couldn't go on the front porch if the mailman was out there. It was really hard for me because

I wanted to be nice to everyone. I was one who wanted to help people if I could. I never had much, but I would give what I had if it didn't take from my children. Jesse wouldn't help anyone unless it would benefit him. The world owed him, in his eyes. I got beat for saying a man on TV was good-looking. Like I could go out and sleep with John Stamos or Patrick Swayze.

Jesse would not let me correct or discipline my children. He taught them early on how to manipulate, disrespect, and blackmail me. He would tell them if I spanked them or got on to them while he was gone, to tell him and he'd beat my ass when he got back. What child wouldn't use that? My now oldest son would use that a lot. He told me one day if I didn't give him money, he was going to tell Daddy I spanked him while he was gone and "Daddy will beat your ass." My son was eight years old at the time. Jesse would also tell the boys to tell him if I went outside when any man came over or even if I went on the porch. I told Amos one day that I would call the police and get him for mommy abuse. After he kept on threatening me and cursed me, I picked up the phone, dialed time and temperature, acted like I was talking to the police, and said I wanted to report my son abusing his momma. Amos started crying, "Please, Momma, I am sorry. I will not be mean to you again," but when Jesse got back, Amos told him what had happened, and boy did I get it. I couldn't win for losing.

From the time the kids could walk and talk, Jesse brainwashed them. He would ask them, "Who do you love more, me or Momma?" He also would teach them to pinch Momma's boob and butt. I'd tell him all the time that was sick! You don't teach your sons to grab and pinch their momma on her butt or breast. But he'd just laugh. Jesse would make the boys talk terrible to me or tell them to do things to me, their own momma. My oldest son, Daniel, was the only one who would not talk to me horribly or grab me when Jesse said to. When Jesse would tell him to tell me he didn't love me, to tell me he only loved his daddy, Daniel would cry and say, "No, I love my momma." He was a mama's boy!

Jesse would go sleep with other women. He thought at one time he was the father of one girl's baby, and he bragged about it. The

DNA came back. It wasn't. But he still thought the baby was his. He said it came back 99.9 percent that he wasn't the father, so there was still a chance he was. I always knew he slept around a lot, and that's why he accused me of sleeping with other men. Jesse told my kids growing up that he wasn't their father, but since he raised them, he was. He talked to them like they were his buddies. I hated that. Every other word was the f-word, among every other cuss word and vulgar word in the dictionary. He degraded women all the time in front of them. He had no respect for anyone, so why should his kids? Jesse was going to make sure that I didn't have a normal mother-son or mother-daughter relationship with my children. He was so selfish, only thought about himself and only cared about himself. And that's what he was teaching the kids. And no matter what, you don't admit to anything, and nothing is ever your fault, even if the proof is right there in front of you. Deny, deny, deny!

One day, he beat me, and I tried to run to the neighbor's house for help. He caught me by my hair and pulled the entire left side of my head bald. I think the neighbors heard me screaming and called the police. When the police came, they got me outside and asked what was going on. One officer tried to get Jesse to come outside, but he knew if he did, he was going to jail. He even told them they were stupid if they thought he was stupid enough to come out, because he knew he would go to jail if he stepped out of the house. One officer asked him why he was hitting me. Jesse said, "I never touched that b——. She tripped and fell and I tried to catch her."

One officer said, "Oh, she fell and all her hair came out? And you have all her hair in your hand."

He said, "Yep, you got it. I never touched that b——!" There you go, never admit anything! They finally got him to step out and took him to jail, although they told him he could signature bond out but couldn't return to our house that night. Right! I was so afraid of him and he had threatened me, so when we went to court, I was afraid to press charges. And the judge scolded me and told me he could get me for filing false charges and put me in jail. From then on, I never trusted the court. Could he not see I was terrified of Jesse? Or he just didn't care. Jesse was the son of Satan, yet it always fell back on me. I was the one to blame. Everything was my fault. It was my fault he hit me and done horrible things to me. Jesse beat me weekly, sometimes daily. And he always told me it was my fault for making him mad. He would cuss at me, scream at me, and make me say "Yes, sir." He was far from a sir.

I remember several months later, going to get my haircut, the lady kind of laughed. She said, "This is funny. You have like a bunch of new hair growth all over this one side of your head. Have you done chemo?" I just said I didn't know why it was like that. I couldn't tell this lady what had really happened. It was too embarrassing. I was ashamed after what she said. My life was a nightmare My life was a nightmare I couldn't wake up from. He made sure he alienated me from everyone and my family. Friends were totally out of the question. I was young and so alone. If the court or authorities wouldn't help, who did I have?

Yes, in the very beginning, I left him a few times and should have stayed away from him, but he had this strong hold on me. In the very beginning, I was so naive, scared, and believed he would change, and my children could grow up with both parents. If I had only known. Jesse got away with so much criminally I felt he could kill me and get away with it. He shot his friend in the leg, and because he was afraid of Jesse, Jesse got away with it. They questioned him, but that was all. They knew he done it. So many things he got away with, other than several DUIs and a few theft charges. Jesse was so evil and so selfish. He only thought about himself and only cared about Jesse. Everyone was to give him all the attention, and he was the only one who was to be loved and acknowledged.

He made me get rid of my little dog because she loved me so much, and he knew I loved her. She would sit outside the bathroom door while I was in the bathroom. Jesse wouldn't let me let her in the bathroom with me. She would cry sometimes until I got out. Her name was Missy. She was part weenie and Chihuahua, just the sweetest thing. And because I gave her attention and showed her love, he hated her. He would kick her and be mean to her. He made me drop her off, or he dropped her off because I couldn't, Jesse dropped her off at an exit ramp, beside a house with a fence. I cried for two days.

I loved her so much, and I was worried about her. The third day, he says, "Come on, b——, we'll go back and if she is there, you can get her." He didn't think she'd be there. As we drove up, I seen her still sitting in the same spot he put her. So I jumped out and got her. I paid for it, and I ended up finding her a home later because he was so mean to her. I did find her a good home, but it really hurt me. That was Jesse. I was not to love anyone or anything but him. Such a real selfish ass!

Years later, he would get another dog for me and the kids. Tori was a small Pomeranian, tan and white. After a while of my giving her love and attention and her so attached to me, I had to give up yet another. I found an older couple in the country to take her. But it broke my heart. It wasn't very long after I had to give Tori up that I finally escaped. In the eighties and nineties, abuse wasn't taken seriously, or at least domestic abuse. You didn't hear about it like you do now, and it was hard to get the police to respond when they knew it was a man and wife. One time that the police did respond, because neighbors complained, the officer told me to leave, but he couldn't give me a ride. He didn't take Jesse to jail. I begged the officer to take me to my mom's, but he said he couldn't, that all he could do was follow me a ways away from the apartments. He followed me maybe three blocks and then just took off! Well, I knew Jesse was also following me. Right after the cop took off, Jesse grabbed me. Thank you, Officer!

I was seven months pregnant, and Jesse had already hit me, bit my kneecap so hard because I put my legs up trying to protect my stomach, punched me, and pulled my hair out again! This was all over his sister telling him I talked to a guy in the parking lot, which she done quite often. She was a little off too, if you ask me. She would undress in front of her brothers, mainly Jesse. She would go right in the bathroom when they were in there. And take her shirt and bra off right in front of them. The youngest brother, JR, was the only one to say anything to her. And tell her that was wrong and how ignorant she was. But it didn't stop her. Sometimes I wondered about her and Jesse. And they had a cousin who done the same thing. She had no couth either. Abuse wasn't taken seriously or it seemed that way. And it was like the police treated me like I was stupid, so deal with it. Unless you have been abused, been with an abusive spouse or boyfriend, you don't know how hard it is to get away from that situation. And it's even harder when you have children. The longer a woman is in that situation, the harder it is to get out. And that's if she is lucky enough to get out at all.

Such Evil

I never understood why no one ever helped me when Jesse was beating me. As in his family who was usually around. Like the time we pulled up at his uncle's garage apartment. Jesse had been drinking. He always went to his uncle's for pot. He started accusing me of wanting to sleep with his cousin. He pulled my head down in his lap under the steering wheel. He kept saying, "Tell me, b———. Tell me you want him!" as he punched and pounded my head. The more I told him it wasn't true, the harder he hit me. I can't tell you how many times he punched me in the head that day. I know he hit me for several hours, constantly saying I will not stop until you admit you screwed him. I begged him to please stop; I didn't want anyone else. His cousin was coming down the alley, but when he heard me screaming, he took off. Jesse said, "He knows he's guilty he hauled ass. Now tell me you ——— him!

Scared for my life, I finally said, "Okay, you are right. Please stop, Jesse." But that didn't work. He only became more violent with me. About that time, Jesse's ex-girlfriend came up to the car and asked him what was going on. He said, "I'm going to kill this whore!"

She said something like "Come on, let's go get high."

Jesse grabbed me by my hair and said, "Come on, b———, you are gonna watch me f———her."

I said, "No, you can have her. Let me go."

He said, "Oh no, you are gonna watch and see how it feels. Get up the stairs, b———." He pulled me up the stairs by my hair and threw me on the hide-a-bed. His uncle asked him what was going on. He said, "I'm gonna f——— her in front of her or kill her. He told his uncle to go get his gun. I was terrified. I tried to get out the door, but he caught me. His uncle gets up and goes into his bedroom, with me begging him to help me. I was bloody, my hair was pulled out and all a mess. Why did he just go in the other room? Red did stop him from getting the gun the first time. Jesse pulls out the bed and tells Amy to get undressed, and she does! He pushed me in the floor between the couch bed and wall and said, "You're next, b——."

I thought to myself, *Over my dead body.* I waited for my chance and made a run for it. Red's apartment was in the alley, and there was a house in front. So I took a chance and made it out the door. I ran so fast down the stairs. As I reached the bottom, I heard him behind me. My heart was racing, and I started screaming for help. Jesse tells me to stop or he would shoot me. I wasn't stopping. I made it to the porch of the neighbor's house, still screaming. As I reached the door, Jesse grabbed me! But the man opened the door and told him the police were on their way and he'd better turn me loose. So Jesse did. I just fell into that man's arms. The officer came, but Jesse had already left. He was good at getting away. Just about every police officer in town knew Jesse. But I got lucky that day this was one officer who couldn't stand Jesse and said he didn't understand why this guy was still walking the streets. He gave me a ride to Mom's and warned me to stay away from Jesse. Jesse was no good. If I had only taken his advice!

Empty Promises

I stayed at Mom's a few weeks, until I found out I was pregnant. During the time I was at Mom's, Jesse came around constantly. "I will change. You know it was the whisky. I will stop drinking, I swear, and, baby, you know if you would fight me back and stand up to me I wouldn't do that." Yeah, right! After Jesse wore me down and promised things would be different. "We have a baby coming. That's all I ever wanted," he says. "I'll never hurt you again." That was his famous song. As always, he would do good for a week or two. He got a job. So maybe he was wanting to change? We were staying with his mom until we could get housing assistance. And his two brothers were also living at his mom's, so I couldn't stay there while he was working. So for a while, he made me sit in the car while he was working. Until one day, a supervisor seen me and told Jesse I couldn't be sitting in the parking lot all day. So I had to sit at the park behind the plant.

One day, while waiting for Jesse's lunch break, a man came walking toward me with his penis in his hand. I drove out of there so scared. But of course it was my fault. I must have flirted with him. After that, I had to go back to sitting in the plant parking lot but hunkered down in the floorboard so I wouldn't be seen. Because of all the stress, I ended up losing the baby. Shortly after, I was pregnant again. That's all I ever wanted was a family of my own. I guess because I always had children to babysit, for my mom's boyfriend's sons, and growing up without my dad, I wanted to make sure my kids had both parents. Little did I know or realized that I had picked

Satan. I stayed so stressed the next twenty years and still somewhat today. I am still so easily stressed, and I have bad anxiety issues.

Jesse quit his job about a week later. About a month before the baby was due, he got another job at another chicken plant. So we could get our own place, it was a requirement at the time to be eligible for the housing assistance. Jesse started drinking a lot more. Hell, it was his right. I mean he did get a job and an apartment. I remember I would always start shaking, and my heart would race right before he got home, especially on Fridays. I never knew what mood he was going to be in. If he came home and dinner wasn't what he wanted, it went all over the walls and floor. I spent all day cleaning. The house would be spotless and dinner cooked when he got home, and then to have him throw a fit and throw my food all over the place; he was so very mean and inconsiderate. And if he seen me cry as I cleaned up his mess, he'd start punching me. He threw food a lot and then cuss and hit me because there was a mess. "Clean this. S——— up now you w———!" For many years, my name was bitch and whore.

My Firstborn

When the baby came, Jesse was so jealous of him. I held him too much. I didn't let him cry enough. He's not gonna have a p—— for a son. He was two weeks old! Jesse was at work, and one of his friends came by. I never opened the door. I told him to please leave. Jesse wasn't home, and he needed to leave. My luck! As he was walking down the stairs, Jesse pulled up. I wanted to jump out the window. I heard Jesse ask him what he was doing there and said, "Hey, man, you screwing my wife while I'm at work?" Then he said, "Hell, man, I am just messing you." But he wasn't. Lord, he wasn't. He just didn't want to fight that guy. Not enough liquid courage. My heart was racing, and my insides were shaking so hard. Jesse kicked the door. "What the f——, b——? You f—— him, you whore!"

I started crying. Daniel started crying, but Jesse wouldn't let me pick him up. "Don't you dare touch that little bastard!"

I said, "He's hungry, please…"

"No, you don't touch him."

I kept trying to go pick him up, but Jesse wasn't having it. I begged him. He said, "I'm sick of you babying that mf. Jesse had been drinking already. He went to the kitchen and got a knife. I was so terrified. He said, "You love me? Prove it. Stab that little SOB."

I cried, "Jesse, please, he's our baby." I didn't know what else to do. I needed help. I knew he wouldn't hurt Daniel. So I made a run for it. I ran so fast and hard two blocks to the little store and called Mom to help me. She said she would bring the police to stay put. While waiting for Mom and the police, Jesse pulled up at the store. I asked him where Daniel was. He said he's at home and I'd better get in the car. I tried to stall, but he kept getting irate. So I went to get in the car, but every time I tried, he gunned the engine like he was going to run me over. "Okay, I'll quit," he said, laughing. "Get in." And he'd rev the engine again and lunged forward like to run me over. Finally, I got in and was praying Mom and the police would show up. We got back to the house. As Jesse was walking upstairs, the police came with Mom. She didn't have a car. We finally got Daniel, and the officer drove us to Mom's. What father is jealous of their own son and tries to make you stab him? Of course, Jesse claimed he was only kidding around. He was testing me to see if I would hurt his son. He was truly jealous of Daniel. Jesse wanted all the attention all the time. Jesse was so jealous of all my children. He hated it if they showed me love or if I showed them love.

Drinking and Drugs

I am not perfect. I have made mistakes. I'll be the first to admit it. But I tried to live right. I never believed in cheating or doing people wrong. Doing things just to benefit me. All I ever wanted was to live right, have a family of my own, and be happy. Although Jesse drank and did drugs, I never liked those things. Jesse tried to get me to all the time, but I was afraid of it, thank God! I remember one time he got so mad because I wouldn't drink and smoke pot with him. I took two puffs off his marijuana, and I freaked out. I remember I couldn't see, my head was spinning, and I thought I was going to die. I started crying because I was so scared. I begged him to take me to the hospital. His sister was staying the night with us. He had to have someone to drink with him. As I went to the kitchen to get him another whisky and coke, I remember looking at her, and it looked like she was laughing at me in slow motion. I made Jesse a drink and went back to the bedroom and begged him again to please take me to the hospital. He said, "Are you f—— crazy? They will know I got you high." I told him to just drop me off; they wouldn't have to know about him.

He thought it was so funny when someone got so high and started to freak out. It was hilarious to him. I guess because he could handle a lot of drugs and alcohol, and it was a game to him to see who could get the highest, or do the most drugs. But he wouldn't let me go. I think that was a blessing from God. If I wasn't against drugs before, this definitely sealed it. I remember having nightmares for years of me being high, driving a car, and not being able to see where I was going. At this time, we didn't have kids yet. From that day forward, I learned how to fake smoking and I wasted a lot of his pot and alcohol. Ha-ha! I could do Mr. Roper from *Three's Company* real well. Turn my head and slowly blow out smoke without inhaling. I got so good at it.

Jesse always had to have his brothers or cousin around to drink and get high with. They would drive around drinking and smoking and see some guy walking alone on the side of the road. They would pull over, get out, and ask him if he had money or drugs, then they would all beat the guy half to death. I seen it happen several times. I made the mistake one time of telling him he was a wimp. "It takes three or four of you to jump one little guy. It takes a bigger man to walk away." Boy, did he beat me then. And again, his brothers and cousin did nothing!

Mom always told me a man who beats a woman is a coward. He wouldn't fight one-on-one and he'd rather hit a woman as a man. And she was so right. She told me it takes a bigger man to walk away, and I never forgot that. I learned to keep it to myself. Like I said, Jesse had to have someone to drink with. When he couldn't get his brother or cousin, he'd ask a friend. He invites them to party with him, then after they got drunk, he'd accuse me and the friend of wanting to screw if the guy looked at me or he thought I looked at him. Jesse blamed his rage on the drugs and alcohol but only continued to drink and do more drugs. He would also blame me. I made him mad. I made him hit me. That is no excuse. But it is every abuser's song. "You made me do it."

So Horrible to Everyone

One night, Jesse and a friend were drinking. He asked him, "Why do you keep looking at my wife?"

He said, "Jesse, man, I'm not. I don't want your wife, dude."

Jesse picked up a thick, heavy drinking mug, got up in the guy's face, and said, "You think I'm f—— stupid?"

The guy said, "No, man" and laughed.

Jesse said, "Well, is this f—— funny" and hit him hard enough to shatter that mug over his head. All I saw was his head open up and more blood than I think I've ever seen. We were at his sister's house. She was drinking with them. I think that sobered her up. She got mad, jumped Jesse, and told him to leave. She was calling the police and an ambulance. The guy passed out. Jesse's sister thought he was dead. She called 911, but Jesse didn't leave until we heard the sirens, and then he panicked. He left without me and the kids. You could hear the tires squeal. I know the cops had to have heard him. Luckily, the guy wasn't dead. The paramedics said he hit him just right and with all the alcohol he'd drunk, he was on the verge of passing out anyway. They couldn't give the guy anything at the hospital until his alcohol level came down. And of course, Jesse got away with that. The guy stayed away for a couple months, but eventually, he came back around. And they got drunk together again and talked and laughed about it. Everything was always funny to Jesse, unless it happened to him, and then the whole world better stop for him.

Jesse could do so much and get away with it. He had cop friends who themselves broke the law. I saw so much, but what could I do? They wore a badge. Thankfully, I haven't heard their names in a long time. I really hope they are off the force. Jesse stayed away all night thinking the police were watching him. I got a good night's sleep that night.

Lazy and Disrespectful

Jesse wouldn't work, so we spent the first several years living with his family. We would get a place but lose our assistance because he wouldn't comply and look for employment. His meaning of work was mowing lawns enough to get his drugs and alcohol. I can't tell you how many times we moved, but I do remember moving like six times in one year because we couldn't pay rent. It was especially hard and heartbreaking for me after we had kids, not ever being at one place long enough for them to call home. Or spending days in our car. I was too ashamed to tell my family. Jesse had alienated me from my family. My family wanted nothing to do with him. They tried to tell me to get away from him. They always wanted me to leave him. I wasn't allowed to work. There were men, and I think he was afraid I would tell someone what he does or someone would help me get away.

I was in the hospital having our second son, Amos. Jesse never stayed in my room long at all. It really made me nervous too. His uncle Butch came to see Amos one day, and Jesse hadn't even been to the hospital yet, or as far as I knew, he hadn't. He always accused me of sleeping with everyone, and he didn't like his uncle Butch, so my heart was racing. Butch asked where Jesse was. I told him Jesse hasn't been there yet that day. I really wanted to tell him to leave because I knew Jesse would think we were screwing around. I remember praying he would leave before Jesse got there. But as my luck would have it, Jesse walked through the door. He asked Butch what he was doing. He said, "I just came to see the baby and congratulate you."

Jesse said the baby is in the nursery. He wasn't rude and even told his uncle he'd walk down to the nursery with him. I remember wondering what was up with him, only to discover later one of his ex-girlfriends was in the room next to me. She just had her second child. He was spending a lot of time in her room when her husband wasn't around. And after that, that was another excuse to beat me. Accusing me of screwing his uncle. Jesse's brother, Jon, came up to the hospital and walked in my room. He said, "Jesse, did you see the name on the room next door?"

Jesse said, "Shut up, man, yeah I did and it's her. I went in and seen her."

I was like, "Really?"

He said, "You know she was my first love. I had to see and she still looks hot. A little fat but hot." He had no respect for me, his baby, or that girl. I also found out a week or so later he was talking to her every day, trying to meet her. They were planning a day to get together. She would call all the time and hang up if I answered. He invited her and her husband over for dinner and drinks, in an attempt to get to sleep with her. And he finally succeeded. He went out drinking one night and called me, threatening me, telling me he was coming home to beat my a———. He brought up his uncle at the hospital to scare me into leaving. Then Tina's husband called looking for her. He had their kids, and she never came home. He also knew she was with Jesse. I ended up taking a cab to their place so he could go find her. He found them at my house. Jesse done things like that all the time. But it always ended up being my fault. He seen her a few times here and there, and they ended up getting married years later after I finally got away from him. And of course, I would get accused of screwing Tina's husband.

Harder to Escape

The longer we were together, the more I grew to really hate him. It got harder to get away from him because we had kids. Jesse always told me I would never leave him, I would never get away with his children. I fantasized all the time of the day my children and I would get away from him. But I would also get so nervous just thinking about it. Jesse told me many, many times he'd kill me before I left him, and I truly believed him. I would fantasize about killing him, but even just the thought would cause a panic attack. I would think if I missed or if he got up. And I never in my life wanted to hurt anyone. But at times, it came across my mind.

He'd say, "No court would ever let you just leave with my kids." After everything he had gotten away with, I believed it. It was like the court just brushed him under a rug so they didn't have to deal with him. That is the effect he had on people. He got so many chances from the police before he was charged with anything. He had so many DUIs he should have gone to prison. But he knew people who worked for the court. Every cop at that time knew Jesse well. They all hated to see him and deal with him. He had finally gotten enough DUIs and theft charges, he was facing a few years in prison. I couldn't wait! That was my ticket to freedom! But when my son died, the prosecutor said they didn't have the heart to send him down. Just my freaking luck! Really! Didn't have the heart? I am so cursed!

Jesse was just evil. I mean what husband or dad does the things he had done? I can't count the times he'd be drinking. We'd have a newborn baby, he'd drive crazy and so fast through town, not stopping at stop signs and pulling out in front of cars. One night, or morning, about three o'clock, my daughter was two weeks old. Jesse threw a fit because he didn't have any pot. He left the boys with his drunk brother. They were asleep, but still. He made me go with him and bring Danielle. He wanted me to ask people for pot for him. He drove like a bat out of hell from one town to the other, not stopping at all, and pulled out in front of a semitruck. How we didn't get hit was a wonder. I kept begging him to let me drive. Did he not care about his daughter?

"I'm just having f—— fun, b*——."

I said, "You are going to get us killed!" He punched me in the face and floored it. Laughing his butt off. He went by a few houses asking for a joint, but no one would give him anything. He became irate at that point. Honestly, I don't know how we made it home. I know he drove like a maniac, and I prayed for a cop to see him. I mean at three in the morning, not too many people were out. Where were the police when I needed them? It was always my fault when he couldn't get drunk or high. But everything was my fault, no matter what. I never knew what mood Jesse would be in when he got home, or got up in the morning, for that matter. He was like a light switch, smiling one minute and beating me the next.

No One to Turn To

In 1991, I had four boys—Daniel, Amos, Andrew, and Ray. Ray was born in February. And my daughter was born December of 1991. It was a really bad year. It was late June. We were waiting on our housing and utility assistance to kick in. Our electricity got shut off. It was the hottest June ever, I believe. Even the nights were so hot you couldn't sleep. I would sponge bathe the boys, with cold water of course, but I figured it would cool them off and help them sleep. We made them a pallet on the living room floor by the front door to try and get some kind of breeze. I remember rubbing one of the boys' head, and I felt something wet. So I felt around, and the pallet was also wet. I got the candle so I could see if it was sweat or what. The boys had gotten so hot they threw up and went back to sleep in it. I lost it. I cleaned them up, crying the entire time. "What are we gonna do, Jesse?" He told me to get the kids in the car and drive around to cool them off. Well, we may have had a quarter tank of gas. Jesse told me to go to his sister's or mine and see if the kids and I could stay the night. That was the only time I really asked anyone for help, but my babies needed it.

Jesse had really alienated everyone. He was such an ass nobody wanted anything to do with him, and so they didn't want me or my kids around either. I went to a few places that night asking for a place for the night for my children and myself. Nobody would let us. This was unreal. My own family wouldn't allow my children, their nephews, to stay one freaking night because they hated Jesse. So I begged, "Please let my kids in for the night. I will sleep in the car," but no. I knew at point I was totally on my own. I wouldn't ask anyone for a damn thing ever! Mom had just gotten married, and she lived an hour and a half away. And I never liked asking her for anything or letting her know how bad my life was. I mean she tried to get me to leave Jesse so many times. I didn't want her to know he beat me and he was too lazy to work and support his kids. I drove back to my apartment because I had nowhere else to go, and I was driving on fumes. I cried all night long. I guess the apartment manager heard me, and he dropped an extension cord down from his apartment and said, "Maybe with this you can plug in the refrigerator and a couple of fans." He was godsent, let me tell you. He let us use that cord until we moved a week later. So I thought things would start looking up. We finally got rental and utility assistance, so I know the kids would have a roof and electricity. We found a duplex through a realtor.

The Death of My Son

I was pregnant with my fifth child. Daniel and I would watch *Rescue 911* together. He was a mama's boy. We'd snuggle on the couch all the time when Jesse was gone. We didn't know yet what I was having. Daniel would say, "Momma, I want a sissy. I am sick of bubbas," then he'd rub my belly. One night, watching *Rescue 911*, it was a story of a pregnant woman in trouble, and they had to do a C-section. He said, "Momma, how are they gonna get that baby out of that momma?"

I said, "Well, honey, they will have to cut her belly."

He said, "If they cut her belly, they will cut that baby. Don't let the doctors cut your belly or they will cut my baby." He was so sweet and so smart. Anytime we were out, he would flirt with women. They just loved him. One day, getting my tags on my car, Daniel was winking or blinking both eyes at the ladies behind the counter. They both started laughing and smiling, saying, "He is so precious and we believe he is flirting with us. He is going to be a ladies' man." He just kept blinking both eyes at them. It was so cute. He was flirting.

It was September of 1991. The boys went to my mom's for the weekend. She wanted to take them to the fair. Daniel turned four on September 16. Mom brought the boys home on September 26. They had a great time. Mom took a picture of Daniel, Amos, and Lee, my oldest nephew, and put it in a tiny frame for Daniel. Like a 2x2. Daniel loved that picture. He wouldn't leave it on the shelf. He kept taking it and putting it in his pocket. He also had one pair of jeans he was crazy about. I had a hard time getting him out of them to wash. The morning of the twenty-eighth, I got up with the boys. It was a Saturday. The boys were watching cartoons. Jesse had been out all night drinking and passed out on the living room floor. His youngest brother, JR, stayed with us, and he was asleep in the boys' room.

I went to get the boys' clothes, and as I came down the hall, all I seen was flames coming from behind the couch. I remember screaming for Jesse to help. I told Jesse to get the boys out of the house, but he went to move our car from the carport. Ray was in his walker. I grabbed Ray and ran to get JR up, screaming. As I turned around, the entire house was full of smoke and flames. I grabbed the boys and put them in the backyard. It's still all a blur. I just remember turning around and Daniel was gone. I couldn't find him. There were people everywhere. It was like I was in a tunnel. I couldn't hear well, and I couldn't find my baby. I was screaming for someone to please help! "Please get my baby! Help me!" I remember people telling me to sit on the ground. Ray had some heat burns on his face. A woman had taken him to her house and changed him and put something on his face and brought him to me. Another lady, who was our neighbor and her husband knew my Mom, came up to me and asked for Mom's phone number so she could call her for me. I remember screaming and cursing at the firemen to go in and get my baby. The next thing I remember, two guys were carrying me, one on each side of me. I was sitting Indian style, holding my boys, and that's how they carried me because they wanted me out of there and I wouldn't go. They carried me two blocks like that. I remember I threw up in the lady's flower bed. She told me my mom was on the phone and wanted to talk to me. I will never in my life forget my mom's scream! I can still hear it today.

I remember the fire chief coming in and telling me I needed to hush and listen. I screamed, "NO!" I knew what he was going to tell me. Lord, this had to be a nightmare. Please wake me up, God, please! I remember saying to Mom, "Momma, my baby, Daniel." They made me go to the hospital to get checked out since I was pregnant and kept me overnight. I had inhaled some smoke. From this point on, there was nothing Jesse could do to hurt me. This was such unbearable pain I wouldn't wish on anybody. The firemen told me they found Daniel holding his puppy. We had just gotten Daniel and Amos a puppy. Daniel loved his puppy, Duke. I can't remember the other one's name.

I remember there was a guy, a bald man, who kept trying to go in and get Daniel. I remember seeing him leaned up against the tree before the men carried me down the road. I tried to find that man, find out who he was to thank him for risking his life, but nobody knew him or who he was. I was told he didn't want to be known, and it really bothered him that he didn't get Daniel out. Why have I been so cursed? Everyone fought over who we would stay with. Two months earlier, nobody wanted me or my kids around. I will never forget the phone call to the realtor to tell her about the duplex. When I told her we had a fire and I lost my baby, she said, "Well, you worry about your loss and I will worry about mine."

I said, "Lady, you can replace your house. I can't get my baby back." She just hung up. I hate to say I was not that nice when saying that to her, but she treated the loss of my baby boy like he was property, not a human being. A few weeks later, my sister and I went back to our house. She said she'd go in to see if there was anything of Daniel's salvageable I could have. She went on our side. She found his favorite pants with the little picture in them. I went on the neighbor's side, and it was so odd. There wasn't as much as a canned food left. It was totally empty. The bathroom mirror/medicine cabinet was melted to the wall. But when we pried it open, it too was empty. I noticed during the fire, they had a truck in the driveway packed high with their belongings on it. It always made me wonder.

I couldn't watch the news or read it in the paper. But Mom was furious with our local paper. They wrote, "It was found under a chair holding its puppy." She made them rewrite it. My son wasn't an *it* for one, and he was behind the chair, not under it. People are so cruel and heartless.

The Letter from God

You never ever get over losing a child. We ended up staying with Jesse's mom until we got a place. One day, in the mail was a letter addressed to Jesse, and the return address had "G.O.D." I remember feeling hurt after reading it, thinking, *Where is my letter?* I felt this was God letting me know he was okay and a sign for Jesse to straighten up. Although Jesse didn't it see it that way. Like always, it was someone attacking him, and the truth always pissed him off. I had that letter for years, then it was stolen when my house was broken into. The letter, as I remember, read

> Dear Daddy, I just want you to know I am in Heaven with Jesus and I am okay. Please tell Momma not to cry. Daddy it really hurts me when you get drunk and beat my Momma and yell at my brothers. Daddy please don't hurt Momma anymore. I Love you Daddy tell my Momma I am okay and I Love her. Love Daniel

I wanted a letter from Daniel. He was my son, my baby, momma's boy. Of course Jesse got mad. "This is from your f—— momma! It is typed, and it's something she would say."

I said, "No, my mom would never send something like that. She'd know something like this would really hurt me." Jesse acted like he was the only one suffering. And he tried to use it to his benefit, to make everyone feel sorry for him. He tried taking the letter to the police and seeing if they could get fingerprints. He wanted someone arrested for sending it, mainly my mother. Oh, he couldn't stand the truth or for anyone to call him out on something, because he was never wrong, nor did he do wrong. But I never told Mom all Jesse had done to me over the years. I never told anyone all Jesse had done to me. To Jesse, it was only an attack toward him. God couldn't send a letter.

My Hell Continued

We moved into our own place, thanks to the Red Cross. But for the longest time, I thought I was going crazy. I heard Daniel walking and jumping around in the boys' room all the time. And I think Amos did too, because he wouldn't go into his room and play. He'd cry. It took a really long time for Amos to be able to play in his room. Jesse tried to make him go in his room and play all the time, calling him a little p———.But I'd tell Amos it was okay, he could stay in the living room with Momma. December 24, 1991, I had Danielle. Only three months after Daniel died. That was supposed to be my happy moment. I waited on a little girl for years. Don't get me wrong—I was happy, but still so sad. I found out two weeks before Daniel died that I was having a girl. He was so happy. He would rub my belly all the time and talk to her. I named her after him.

Jesse still hadn't changed. I thought Daniel dying would make him change, but for a while, he got worse. He drank more. He never took up for me at all, or his children, for that matter. He had parties all the time. I hated it. He couldn't drink or smoke pot without having his buddies or brothers over. He would let his stepbrother, Shawn, and his brother JR drink and smoke pot even though they were underage. One night, he had the guys over. Danielle was two weeks old. They would listen to loud music and curse each other, talk crap to each other. They thought it was funny. I hated my kids to be around that. And it scared me, because if I looked too long or talked to one of them, Jesse would hit me.

So that night, they were messing with Jesse's brother Jon, talking crap to him because he was like twenty-four and still a virgin.

I don't remember exactly what was said, but it was kinda funny, so I laughed. I didn't laugh much. Jon looked at me and said, "Heee, Daniel is dead. Is that funny?" I lost it and threw an ashtray at him. Well, instead of getting mad at the remark he made about our son we just lost, Jesse got up and started punching me in the head. Never said a word to Jon for what he said. Well, the more he hit me, the madder he got and the more he hit. Then he started throwing stuff. Well, his cousin said, "Come on, Jesse, she's holding your baby and Jon was in the wrong."

Well, that really pissed Jesse off. "What, man, you want to f—— her, is that why you are taking up for her?" Well, as usual, they all got up and left. Danielle was crying, I was crying, the boys woke up. Jesse took off, but I knew when he got back, depending on his mood, he'd either wake me up choking and hitting me or pass out. I think I was more hurt that he didn't take up for our son and get mad at his brother, because his punches I was used to. And after losing my son, he couldn't hurt me any more than the pain I was going through from my baby being gone. Since the guys didn't want to come over for a while after he tried to fight them, Jesse let Shawn and his buddy come over to drink and get high.

One night they were over, Jesse kept on at them, "Come on, you p——, drink some more. Take another hit. You are a p—— if you don't." Well, he got them so drunk and so high I guess Shawn got the munchies. He ate a whole pack of cheese you would think that would bind him up. NOT! This kid crapped literally all over my bathroom. It was like he was still going when he got up, fell back into the bathtub, and tried getting up. It was a sick mess. He had crap all over the back of the wall, the toilet and floor. You could actually see his butt marks on the back of the tub down the bottom and up the other side. His shitty handprints were on the light switch, the door handle, and how, I don't know, but on my front door and chair that sit by my door. I was so freaking mad. I just cried. I had to hold my breath while I cleaned the mess up.

This is crap Jesse done all the time. He thought it was funny to get the boys so drunk and high and watch them throw up. It was a game to him. I had to clean up all the mess. I really hoped that

Shawn's friend would tell his parents, but I guess he never did. And that's why these guys are druggies and alcoholics to this day. Just some more evil crap Jesse done. He really thought he could do whatever he wanted, and it was fine. Apparently so!

Labor Nightmare

I tried to go get my tubes tied. We had five children. Well, four living now. I finally got the state to allow it and pay for it. The morning Mom took me to the hospital to have the procedure, I told her she didn't have to wait. It would be a while, and I'd call her when I was in recovery. Well, I waited and waited. The doctor came in and said they needed to do more blood work. The test came back high, meaning I was pregnant. I said, "Oh no, whatever you do, don't tell my mom." Well, it took forever for the second test. My luck, Mom got back early. She was sitting in a chair kind of behind the curtain, it was hard to see her. The doctor came in and said he was right. The second test came back even higher. "You are pregnant."

Mom said, "No! If the ignorant state would have got this done sooner. She is pretty much raising four kids on her own now. Her so-called husband is no help."

The doctor said, "I am sorry. It is what it is." So eight months later, I had baby number six. Another boy, Brennon. I don't know why I was treated like I was by a lot of men. Doctors, lawyers, a judge. I was so cursed when it came to men. I kind of think it was because I was intimidated by men. Scared of men for years. I never could say what was on my mind. I guess in fear of getting beat. There was one doctor who wasn't my doctor at the clinic who would always try to get me to be his patient. I would just smile and tell him I was happy with my doctor, sorry. It seemed like he would always know when I was going to the lab. He showed up every time. About a week before I had Brennon, he saw me in the hall and asked how I was, and he knew it was getting close to delivery date. I said, "Yes, and I am ready."

He said, "Well, don't you worry, I will be there when you have this baby."

I was like, *Yeah right, my own doctor isn't ever there.* About a week or so later, I went into labor. And of course, my doctor's wife was also in labor. So he came in to tell me he would have another doctor take over. Well, guess who came in. Dr. Rite. He said, "I told you I would be here," and smiled. It was a nightmare in itself. Mom was there with me. Somehow, Brennon was under my pelvic bone and would not move. So Dr. Rite tried for hours! Different things to pull him, suck him, turn him. He did a fourth-degree episiotomy and then still tried to use forceps, suction things. They had me on my hands and knees. I was so freaking weak.

I kept begging them to knock me out. "I CAN'T TAKE ANY MORE!" I looked over at Mom, and her face was as white as the sheets, and by the look on her face, I knew something was really wrong. She was on the phone and crying. The nurse was holding my hand and kissing my forehead, telling me, "Hold on, baby." I saw a tray of medical supplies, needles, scalpel, and whatnot.

I told the nurse to give me that scalpel. "I can't take it anymore!"

She told Dr. Rite, "That's enough. This girl is in distress and the baby too. Enough is enough!" I remember blood was everywhere. Mom was freaking out. Finally, they decided to take me to surgery. After eighteen hours of pushing and torture. I remember the anesthesiologist putting the mask on my face, and I started breathing really deep and fast. I wanted to go out.

He said, "Slow down, honey, the gas isn't on yet. We are not ready." I remember crying "hurry," and that was it until I woke up. As I was waking up, someone had a pen in my hand telling me I needed to sign this.

I said, "I can't even see."

A lady said, "It's okay, I'll help you." Well, she pretty much used my hand to sign it. I couldn't see, much less write. I almost lost him. He wasn't breathing for seven minutes. But they finally brought him back, thank the Lord. I remember for days I was real weak and couldn't stay awake. My sister said we were talking and I would pass out, and when I woke up, I finished where I had left off. I had lost so much blood. They ended up giving me a few bags of blood. I remember I was so nervous about that. It was three days before I could hold Brennon. I had nurses come in my room to check my dressings and then ask me if they could bring another nurse in to look. They had never seen anything like this before. I asked one nurse what was the big deal.

She said, "Honey, they cut you really bad and your whooha doesn't even look normal." She said she had only heard of a fourth-degree episiotomy one time in like California, but she thought mine was a severe case. And she'd never heard of doing a fourth-degree episiotomy and a C-section at the same time. That's how my luck is, though. When and if it would or could happen, boy, it happened to me. I'll never forget Dr. Rite coming in my room.

He said, "I just wanted to see how you were. What hurts worse, your twat or tummy? I was trying to save you from a scar so you could still wear your bikini. Do you still love me?"

I said, "Well, I am not allowed to wear a bikini or bathing suit." I just looked at him with tears flowing. A year or so later, he was charged with sexual harassment or something to that effect. Three women took him to court. All I ever heard was he lost his license or couldn't practice in my area. Just my luck to get another creep! I tried to sue him. But after my attorney died, the case was dropped. Yes, I was cursed. I always seemed to draw the creeps out. The ones who made me feel like it was my own fault. The ones who really intimidated me and seemed to take Jesse's side. He had used nondissolving stitches. I guess because he had cut me so bad, he wanted to make sure it had time to heal, I really don't know.

I had to undergo a partial hysterectomy about eight or nine months later. At that time, they removed a lot of the stitches. But I would end up having several more surgeries years later to remove more stitches, scar tissue and untangle my organs. In 2009, I had a four-hour surgery to remove stitches, scar tissue, and a huge fibroid tumor, the size of a grapefruit, on the only ovary I had left, that had all intertwined, and everything had adhered to my stomach lining.

The surgeon said it was a real mess and a tough job for her and her colleague. I would continue to undergo a few more surgeries due to scar tissue and fibroid tumors. My latest surgery was in 2014. I had several more tumors and also had to have part of my colon removed. And more scar tissue removed. I pray all the time the scar tissue doesn't grow back again.

The Hate Really Grew

By the time I had Brennon, I was so miserable. I hated my life, and more so, I hated Jesse to the point I had even thought of suicide as an option to get away from him. Had it not been for my children, I probably would have. The next four or five years, all I did was dream and fantasize about getting away from him, how me and my children's lives would be away from Jesse, although my fantasies were never revealed. A judge was taking Jesse's side and treating me like a criminal. It only showed me that there is no justice whatsoever in the world. I never dreamed a judge would side with Jesse and treat me so horribly, unjustly, and just so wrong.

My happy times were watching Lifetime with Danielle. We would curl up together, watch movies, and now and then peek at each other to see if the other one was crying on a sad movie. As we looked at each other wiping tears, we would laugh. I'd tell Danielle, "It's okay to cry, honey. That just means you have a good heart." Jesse had the boys in the living room with him all the time, playing video games. They would stay up late playing games, no matter if it was a school night or not. Because "I'm the man," Jesse would say. He'd bet money with his friends that Ray could beat them in a game. I will have to say since he was two, he was really good at the games, and most of the time, he would beat Jesse's friends and brothers. I didn't like it. I hated those guys coming over. I hated the boys being able to stay up late playing the games and watching the guys drink, smoke pot, and curse worse than a sailor.

Jesse treated them like friends more than his sons. And letting them do pretty much whatever they wanted really pissed me off, but there was nothing I could do. If I tried to say anything, he would let the boys do more just to spite me, but hurting them more. And Jesse would really get pissed if they beat him in the games. He spanked Ray really hard one time over him beating him in a game. The longer it went on, the less they respected me and the more they tried to intimidate me like Jesse did. And because Jesse would laugh at them, it only got worse. Not only would they talk horribly to me, but they started trying to blackmail me. "If you don't let me, or if you don't give me, I will tell Daddy and he'll beat your ass when he gets home."

I finally realized that Jesse's courage came from a bottle. Either alcohol or pills. Other than with women, Jesse never fought another guy unless he was drunk or hyped up on pills. And it made me sick. Like the time his piece of crap cousin Bill came by after just getting out of prison like the fifth time. They were smoking pot, of course. Jesse was terrified of storms, and if it came up a cloud, we had to go to the hospital basement all night. I hated those nights. He would make the boys sleep in their clothes and shoes if he knew a storm was coming. That night Bill came by, we were getting ready to go to the hospital because there was a storm coming. I used to dream of tying him up in the middle of a field during a tornado and watch him have an anxiety attack and fear for his life and see how it feels.

Bill was messing with the boys, as usual. As I walked in the living room with my shoes in my hand, Bill was on the floor on top of Brennon, and Brennon screamed. I said, "Get your ass off of my son, you freak!" He got up and sat on the couch. Brennon was crying. I asked him what happened. When he told me Bill bit him, I lost it. He left a bite mark on Brennon's face! I hit him up side his head with my shoes, told him not to ever touch my kid again or I'll make sure he goes back to prison. But it wasn't Bills fault. Hell no, a thirty-year-old biting a four-year-old was the child's fault for teasing the thirty-year-old. And I got hit over that, for hitting his cousin and not keeping my place.

At this point in my life, I didn't much care. Jesse's punches didn't hurt anymore. I had gotten used to it. What got me is him taking up for the piece of crap who had been sent to prison for beating women and a child, and not taking up for his own son. But he didn't have any liquid courage that day. Pot wasn't enough to make him courageous. I believe it was after that I tried to plan my escape. But somehow, Jesse knew, or he felt it. He sure made it so hard for me to leave the house with the kids. He always wanted to watch them then. And he started having his dealer deliver pills and pot to him so he never had to leave the house much. He started having an affair with Carol, his drug dealer. I was happy about it. I thought she'd take him from me, but he wouldn't go for it. He wanted her on the side, and it was only to get free dope, or so he said. But with her on the side, maybe he wouldn't bother me. And she was the same; she wanted Jesse on the side. Her husband worked and made good money. She wasn't going to leave that money. She didn't work. Just sold her drugs.

Final Days with Satan

The next year or so was really getting to me. Was I ever going to be free? How can I get my children and myself out of here? I was all alone. I never told anyone what Jesse had done to me the past fifteen years. I was embarrassed, ashamed, and still believed it was my fault. The only people who really knew what Jesse had done to me were his family. And it was like they were all afraid of him. Jesse beat me so many times, and his family never offered to help me. I would escape in Lifetime movies. I watched many, but one movie I'd never forget. *The Burning Bed*. I was on the edge of my seat watching that. It was my life in a movie. I caught myself holding my breath many times. Wanting to jump through the TV and help her. Crying when she finally escaped her evil Satan. I know that was a only movie, but it's real! Women go through hell in the hands of their Satan on a daily basis.

About two years or so before I finally got away from Satan, Jesse's friend had come by. She was telling us about the place where she worked needing help, and she thought it would be a good job for me. Well, Jesse was so different around Loretta. He didn't want her to know he was an evil ass. So he told her, "Yes I think that would be good and with you working the front you can help her." No, what he meant was keep an eye on me. So he asked her all about the job. It was a home for mentally and physically challenged kids and young adults. They ranged from two years to thirty-eight years old. So I started work. It was amazing! I loved it, loved the people and the residents. I would of course go in fifteen minutes early to be sure to be on time. Well, after a short while, Jesse started questioning me why I

ONCE MARRIED TO SATAN

had to go in so early. Who was I seeing before work. What could you do in fifteen minutes or less? He started accusing me of messing with employees. Well, I told him it was all women other than the maintenance crew and we weren't around those guys. So he started accusing me of messing with the residents. These were handicapped people. Most of them were bedridden. But it didn't matter to this sick SOB. So he started taking me and picking me up.

I just loved my job. I got away from him and got to help people. I helped teach sign language to this sweet young girl. She would respond to me, and the head nurse loved it. They had a hard time getting her to try to learn. And she lit up when I came in. But one morning, when Jesse was dropping me off, just so happens the maintenance guy was sitting outside the door, smoking. Jesse went off on him, "You f—— b——! Are you the one f—— my wife? Tell me, you stupid old m——!" I just wanted to hide. Jesse kept going at this guy, and I had never even said as much as *hello* to this man. The man went in the building. Jesse is cussing me now. I wanted to leave. But he said, "Go on, b——. Go on to work. I don't think he'll f—— you today." So shamefully, I went in and clocked in. It was six o'clock. Around nine, when the bosses showed up, I was called in the office and asked to leave, asked to resign. I really hated Jesse more now. I loved that job, and I loved those kids I worked with. I would really miss them. But see Jesse knew I loved that job. I made the mistake of talking good about those kids and letting him know I loved it and loved them. It made me happy.

So I started planning my escape. I packed some clothes and things and put them in the trunk of the car. My excuse was making sure the kids had clothes in case the storms took the house and just in case we had to leave in the middle of the night and not have time to dress the kids. But Jesse told me to take it out of the trunk, he would make sure the kids were dressed. So from then on, my children would go to bed fully dressed when there was a chance of storms. I so tried to play him and get my chance to leave with my children. Jesse kept telling me I would never leave with his kids. "You won't leave alive anyway, you f—— b——." About the last year of my hell, Jesse never would let the kids go with me. I always had to take his sister, Jean, or his mom to the store or doctor. Jean would love to see Jesse hit me. I think she got off on it. She would call him as soon as I dropped her off and tell him I talked to a guy or some guy gave me his number or I just smiled at someone. I was always worried to go home not knowing what she might have told him. Jesse had this way of hitting me and saying, "Heeeee, how was that, b———?" I hated that, the way he'd say it and the stupid look on his face. More so when the boys picked that up. It was all just one big joke to him. He thought he was God's gift and everyone was afraid of him.

I guess Jesse really started feeling my vibes or something. He would make me take a bite off his plate when I made his plate. He thought I was going to poison him. If I had only been that brave. I always wanted to say, "How do you know I didn't just poison that one part." Oh, but I knew better. I thought I had it planned out to get away with my children. I planned to take my sister to get groceries and take the kids because she wanted to see them. But he wouldn't let them go. So I didn't want to go, but I knew he would be suspicious. Talking with my sister, we decided to just go have a night out. Our uncle was playing out, and she wanted to go see him.

I remember her saying, "It will be okay. You deserve it. He goes out all the time." So we did. And we had a good time even though my heart was racing the entire time. When we got ready to leave, I got the car and as I was waiting for my sister to come out, a car pulls up in front of mine. When I seen it was Jesse and his brother, my heart sank! Jesse got out and pulled a gun in my face. I started laying on my horn, and luckily, about that time, my sister and the band walked out the door. Guys started running after Jesse, and his brother about took off without him. There was like fifteen or more guys. Well, I knew I had had it then. I started panicking and didn't know what I was going to do or how I would get my children now. I hoped in a day or so, Jesse would calm down and let me come back. Everyone kept telling me, "Don't worry, the judge will never let Jesse keep the kids. You can get them in court." I never felt real sure about that even though I was and had been a victim all those years. Everyone always seemed to believe Jesse and take his side. He was the poor little victim.

Two days later, I went back and tried to play up to Jesse. I thought it would be okay. I tried to tell him I just needed a night I had never had and how sorry I was and I loved him. About to throw up as I said it. I thought I had him convinced for a minute, but as always, his sister had to call and stir things up. Telling him she'd heard about several guys I slept with. It was such a lie but enough to get Jesse going. He knew the police wouldn't come if he just told them we were fighting. So he calls the police and tells them I was trying to kill him and he feared for his life. Six cop cars showed up. I was not believing this! And as always, they believed Jesse because he had called. There was only one officer out of seven who didn't believe I was trying to kill him, but the one who first responded was an asshole, and he told me I needed to leave or he would arrest me. I said I'd be glad to leave with my children. Jesse and his entire family were telling the cops all kinds of crap.

I looked at the officers and said, "Do I really look like I was trying to kill him?"

"Nevertheless, you need to go right now."

I kept saying, "Not without my kids." I was 110 pounds, which was my standing weight when I wasn't pregnant. Jesse was 180 pounds and muscled up. He worked out a lot, lifting weights, and he was pretty strong.

But the cop said, "You need to leave right now and since you don't have a place to go the kids will remain here. You can take it up with the court."

About that time, Ray came outside on the porch and said, "Yeah, you f—— b——, get out of here. We hate you, you s——."

I just cried. I told the cops, "See what he has my children do? He has beat me for fifteen years, done things to me that's unspeakable, can't you see?"

The one nice officer said, "I know he's putting that boy up to say that they love you, honey, but you'll have to fight it out in court."

I said, "If I leave without my kids he will make sure I never see them."

The officer said, "No, honey. No judge will take a mother's children away." He said he would put remarks in the police report, but it didn't matter! And he never made that report or showed up in court.

So Truly Alone

I was so alone. I couldn't stay with my sister or anyone in my family. I didn't tell Mom what was going on. I didn't really want anyone to know what I had been through the past fifteen years. My sister only knew of what she had seen, which was mild, other than the time I ran to her house trying to get away from Jesse when he was beating me. Only to have her and my brother-in-law turn me over to Jesse when he showed up. They didn't want him around, and he wasn't leaving without me. I remember my heart racing so hard I thought I would have a heart attack. And then hearing them tell him, "Yes, she is here." My heart sank.

I remember seeing a hammer on the table, so I grabbed it, thinking I would try to hit him. But he got it away from me. He said, "What you gonna do, Tam, hit me with a hammer?" And that became a joke on my behalf for years. I had nowhere to go, no money, nothing. I ran into somewhat of a friend. He was actually my sister-in-law's ex-husband. He knew all about that family and hated them.

We got to talking, and he said, "You know you are welcome to stay with me, just roommates. I have a two-bedroom and you could help pay the rent and bills." After a while, I decided, what the hell, I have nowhere to go and no money. I had to be able to get a job and show I could support my children. Everyone I talked to told me not to worry, no judge in his right mind will let Jesse keep your children, you got this! Little did I know how wrong everyone would be. Apparently, I got the judge who wasn't in his right mind, or he was one who didn't like women. It sure seemed that way. Before court, Jesse's dad called me and said we needed to do this right and think of the kids. Try to be civil with one another. I said, "Curt, you don't know the hell I've been through the past fifteen years, nobody does but God."

He said, "Let me take you two to an attorney and do this right where you both can have joint custody of the kids and do it for the kids." If it would mean I could see my children and this would end, I was willing to try.

Abused by the Court System and Judge

My day in court was not my day. It was Jesse's. I didn't have an attorney. I couldn't afford one. So I went to court all alone. Jesse showed up with his sister, my oldest son, Amos, and of course, the attorney I paid. I paid the retainer fee. I was really nervous and could not believe how I was being treated. I really thought I would be able to tell the judge about all the abuse I endured, and he would see what Jesse was and I would get my children. NOT the case at all! That judge treated me like I was a horrible person. It was my own fault for leaving Jesse and like I abandoned my children. Every time I tried to tell him my side, he told me to shut up. He kept telling me to only answer his questions, and every time I tried to say more, he'd say, "That's not what I asked you and if you say more than I ask I can hold you in contempt and put you jail." So belittled by the judge! I was treated like a criminal. I was being abused by the court system who was supposed to protect and serve.

Jesse told the judge I was living with a guy and we were going to get married, and that was not true. I tried to explain to the judge we were just friends and roommates, and he was such an ass! He kept saying, "I said when are you getting married. Do you plan on getting married?"

I was crying and said, "No, sir, I am not."

But he got really mean in his tone and said, "I said when are you getting married?"

I said, "I don't know!"

He said, "Well, let me tell you this, you will not see your children until you get married and bring proof to this court." I was not believing this guy. The judge said since my youngest two children had asthma and I worked all day, he was giving Jesse full custody. He looked at me and said, "Do you have any objections? It wouldn't really matter." I just cried. Amos started crying and left the courtroom. But there wasn't anything I could do. That judge would have put me in jail if I said one more word. Jesse got to the agency who filed my taxes and got my tax refund before court. I was all alone. I had nobody to help me. It was just me in the courtroom on my side. The judge ordered me to go with Jesse and his attorney to the bank and cash my check and give it to Jesse. He did tell his attorney to give me twenty dollars so I could take a cab back to work. He also awarded Jesse child support and told me I owed for the past three months. So I was behind to start with. I will never forget the last words of this judge. He looked at me and said, in a hillbilly accent, "I guess if you are ever able to save up the money, I will see you back in court. I now pronounce you divorced." That's our lovely justice system! The judge did tell Jesse to give me my clothes only. He dropped off a trash bag of clothes at my sister's, but it wasn't my clothes. It was a bag full of size 18W and 22W—a bag of his sister's old clothes.

There Is No Justice

This totally made me lose all hope, respect, and trust in our court system. I would never trust our court system again! That judge degraded me, robbed me of my constitutional rights and abused me just like Jesse, in my opinion. I have always believed that judge was against women as well. And just because you are poor, that doesn't make you a criminal or a piece of shit, as I felt that's how I was treated by him. Because I didn't have an attorney, I wasn't allowed to speak. I had no rights at all. I ended up getting married to my friend just to see my children. I hadn't seen them in six months. But Jesse still wouldn't let me see them for a while. He was going to make sure he totally corrupted them first. When he finally let me see them, I couldn't sleep. I know Jesse put them up to it, but I caught the boys trying to sneak in my room with knives. They all had a big knife. I was scared they would try to stab me in my sleep. And they talked horribly to me. I tried so hard to talk to them and make them understand that sometimes parents just grow apart and can't live together anymore. I tried not to talk crap about Jesse to them. They got enough of that from Jesse. I tried to tell them I just wasn't happy with Dad anymore.

I said, "Aren't you guys tired of the fighting?" Even though it wasn't a fight. It was Jesse beating me and me curling up in a ball to protect myself. But Jesse had already convinced them it was all my fault our family split up. I still never told them all Jesse had done to me over the years, or what he tried to make me do to our son, Daniel. You know I never blamed Jesse for the death of our son. I never blamed God. I blamed myself for years. But the truth is, God took him to save him from the pain. But Jesse always blamed everyone else, even for things he had done and been caught doing. He told my kids it was my fault my baby died, that I let him die because I went to save his brother. God help me!

Jesse would teach my children to steal. I had to hide what little I did have when the kids came over. They had seen all Jesse got away with, and he'd drilled into their heads they can't get into trouble and everyone owes them. No, kids, your dad is the one who owes you. Jesse would still control me the next several years. He'd get me fired from jobs by bringing the kids to my work and sending them in to go wild and act like caged animals. He would sit in the car outside the store where I worked and laugh as they ran around, cursed me, and would take things off the shelves. My boss finally had enough and told me he was so sorry. He knew Jesse was putting the kids up to it, but he couldn't have this in his place of business.

I usually walked everywhere I needed to go. And I would have to put up with Jesse trying to run me over when he seen me. He'd run me into a ditch or up on someone's porch. And the police wouldn't do anything. It was a domestic dispute. File charges, and if he's caught, then they would send him a letter first. If he done it after that and got caught, he'd get a fine. Every job I got, he'd try his hardest to get me fired. So I got a job as a bartender, thinking he couldn't send the kids in a bar. But he tried. Thankfully, I had a good boss who ran Jesse off and told him not to come back or he'd press charges against him. That judge just gave Jesse the legal right to keep my children from me, only let me see them when it would benefit him, and use my children against me.

Locked Up, Alone, and Broken

So I would end up getting a little behind on child support. But I had finally found a job. They were taking child support out of my check. I lived on the street for several months, sleeping in storage units I found open. Finally got an apartment I could afford with the child support I had to pay. I showed up at work one payday, only to be arrested for back child support. Even though the state was withholding child support out of my check, someone forgot to drop the warrant. I was $1,400 behind in child support, but I started out three months behind. They were taking it out of my check, and I still spent thirty-three days in jail. I had no one to call to help me, and I wasn't going to ask anyone anyway, so I had to sit in there through Christmas until I got a court date. So Jesse had another weapon to use to turn my kids more against me. He wasn't going to tell them I was in jail for no reason, or in jail at all. Now he'd really make me look bad by missing Christmas.

So the day I went to court, I get the same judge who helped ruin my life. He says, "What are you doing in jail?"

I said, "You put me here."

He said, "You were working and the state was withholding your support. I'm not sure why you were arrested."

I said, "Me either." He asked me if I thought I still had my job. I said I doubt it. So he said he'd give me sixty days to resume support and ordered the bailiff to release me immediately. But that didn't make up for thirty-three days in jail and losing my job and a place to live. So I was on the street again. I didn't stay with my so-called friend after that. While I was in jail, he had his mother write me a note telling me to sign my paycheck over to help pay the bond. My stupid ass did, and to no surprise, they didn't get me out or even call child support to find out why I had a warrant if they were garnishing my check. This was getting so unbelievable and so overwhelming. I ended up having a nervous breakdown and sent to a facility in Hot Springs, Arkansas. I was taken by ambulance, so when I was released, I was kind of stuck.

I Am Strong and
I Will Survive

Jesse's oldest brother and his family only lived thirty-five minutes from where I was. After walking around most of the day with nothing—no money, no car, no place to sleep—I swallowed my pride and called them. And without hesitation, his wife came and got me. I had a boyfriend at the time who ended up being an asshole. I could tell he had been abusive and used women. Luckily, I got a job, worked most of the time. I was a store manager on salary, so I pretty much lived at work. And Mike got tired of just sitting around. It was out in the country, so no bars or anywhere to go to. Unfortunately, the asshole stole all the money I was saving up to move back home. He stole my shotgun and sold it. But he was gone, and the rest I could get back. My ex-sister and brother-in-law helped me get on my feet, and for that, I will always be grateful to them. They never talked to Jesse or most of the family. They don't agree with all they have done. They done Jesse's older brother very wrong. He worked several jobs to help his family, and they crapped on him. During their last visit while I was still with Jesse, they offered to help me get away, but I didn't want to get them involved, and with it being Jesse's brother, I didn't have much confidence in it.

I finally got back home to be near my children. I had to quit my job to do it. They wouldn't transfer me. The district manager was really upset that I was leaving. I don't blame him. I really turned that store around. Cleaned it up, and the sales had doubled. But I needed to get back close to my kids. I ended up getting a job at a bar. I couldn't take a chance of getting behind on child support again. Although I hated it, it was a job, and if it hadn't been for that job, I wouldn't have met my wonderful husband. I worked days at the bar, which was good. It wasn't as rowdy as nights. A little slow and boring at times, but it paid my bills. My now-husband would come in during the day. He was opening a unique bar in town on a riverboat, and he was looking for bartenders to work for him. He didn't say anything at first. He'd just order and sit at the bar. I would catch him staring at me a lot. He made the comment several times that I didn't seem like a bartender type. Well, the only other bar I worked in was just a beer bar. Beer was easy to sell.

So finally, Marvin asked me if I would be interested in working for him a few nights a week and make some extra money and probably more tips. So I did. I worked both jobs for a while. Then Marvin offered me enough money to be able to quit the other job and just work for him. So we were pretty much together all the time. He also had a business working on the river. He had a couple of tugboats, worked three harbors on the river. So I was his deckhand and copilot during the day and bartender at night. I knew he was a good man, and I will never forget the day he came up behind me and whispered in my ear, "I think I am in love with you." I never dreamed I would find a good man. And then again, I was scared, because he didn't know what hell I had been through, what hell I still had to deal with because of Jesse. But as I slowly told him things, it didn't matter, and he told me from the start I needed to write a book. And the more he found out and witnessed, he couldn't believe I had come from such hell. And the more he encouraged me to write.

Marvin had witnessed a lot during our court proceedings, and he knew all I had told him was the truth. He seen how the court treated me and how Jesse was still getting away with stuff. At one court appearance, Jesse was so high, a blind man could see it. He was tweaking his butt off. The bailiff told him many times to shut up and sit down. He finally asked him what he was on. Jesse said he wasn't on anything. He got bit by a spider on his balls, and he was having a reaction from the antibiotics they gave him. The bailiff said, "I am not stupid. You are high on meth or something and if you don't sit down and be quiet, I will charge you with being under the influence." Okay, really? If it had been me, I would have been in jail. It is illegal to be under the influence in a public place, in a courthouse for sure. Still getting away with everything. Still the poor victim.

Still Battling Satan

Nobody ever believed me when I told them what happened in court. No judge would do that to a mother. It wasn't until Marvin had gone to a few court hearings with me and seen and heard for himself how I was treated and how they all felt so sorry for Jesse. He couldn't believe the court was on his side. Jesse failed several drug tests, and yet the court said he was stressed! It was okay. Marvin and I both were in the random drug testing for the corps of engineers, yet when we took a drug test for the court, at first, they said I failed mine. I was like, Oh, hell no, I didn't."

So then they said, "Oh, we got them mixed up. It was you, Marvin."

He said, "Try again, people. All I will test for is Bud Light. I have never in my life tried pot." If I was involved in it, it would always be chaotic. I never understood what Jesse had told the courts to make them hate me and turn against me like they did. It was embarrassing at first for Marvin to go to court with me, but I finally had a witness to prove how mistreated I was. Why it took until then for anyone to believe me, I'll never understand. I am truly so cursed and jinxed!

Jesse believed I was now rich. Because I had a husband who worked all the time, we paid our bills, and he had a business, so he must be rich. Jesse started having my own kids rob us. They would wait until we were gone and break into our house, stealing little things at first they could sell, or money from our change jar. They broke into our house like five times within two months. They were searching for our safe key and getting what they could along the way. We knew it was the kids and Jesse was behind it. And the kids figured since I was their mother, they wouldn't get into trouble. If I could have proved it, they would have gotten into trouble. Stealing is wrong against the law, and how dare they do this. Marvin worked his ass off to get what little we had, what he had before me. And I worked hard too. So somehow, Brennon, who had stayed with us for a while, found the extra key to our safe and waited for us to be gone. They pretty much knew when we were gone working a boat. We would be gone a while. And it took forever for the police to come, if they came at all. They always had a hard time finding our house for some reason.

We worked in New Orleans when Katrina hit. We took all of his boats and barges down. Ended up selling them to help New Orleans. Which was sad selling my father-in-law's boat he built. While in New Orleans, I bought a nice camcorder, very cheap. I used it to videotape our trip down to New Orleans—the boats and barges, the canal job we done before selling everything. Pretty much wanted some memories of the boats and last job. Only to have the camera and all tapes I made stolen along with several thousand dollars in our safe, which was not ours. Way to go, Jesse. You really taught your children well. It was a punch in the stomach to me. I was so hurt and so embarrassed. And after everything my kids done to us, done to my husband, he still bent over backward to help them. We knew it was my kids breaking in and robbing us, and Jesse was putting them up to it.

Never Held Accountable

Marvin told Jesse after that, if he brought the boys over to rob us one more time, he was going to kick his ass. And meant it. I was afraid to leave my house, and we got robbed several times, broke into several times, yet Marvin goes to jail and has to pay a fine. That's my luck! In court, the judge asked Marvin if he threatened Jesse. Marvin said, "No, sir, I made him a promise if he brought those kids over to rob us one more time, I will kick his ass, and I mean it."

The judge kinda laughed and said, "I will give you time served, but you will have to pay the fine. And stay away from Jesse," and he told Jesse to stay away and not call us. And once again, it was like they didn't want to catch Jesse. They didn't want to have to deal with him. So just let him do whatever he wants. I remember several times Jesse outran the police. I never understood how he got away. One day, we were driving around, Jesse was drinking, and there were two young girls walking down the road. They must have been thirteen or fourteen years old. Jesse pulls over to the side of the road and rolls the window down. He asks them if they want to go f———. About that time, I seen a cop car behind us. Jesse takes off. I see the cop talking to the girls and then his lights came on. Jesse drove as fast as that car would go. Spinning out, cutting sharp corners, and turning sharp one way, then the other. I just knew we would wreck. All you could see behind us was dust. After a little bit, he lost the cop. I just couldn't believe it. Jesse had outrun the cops several times. He never had legal tags or insurance. He'd just go steal another license plate off a car. I told him that was like trying to rape those girls, that he could get serious charges. But he'd laugh and say they can't touch him, he's the man.

Jesse never was held accountable for anything he had done. He got away with everything. He was the problem, yet he was always the victim. Not long after I got away from him, his second wife would call me or come see me asking for help. Jesse had split her face open several times. He beat her with a Weed eater, a baseball bat and threw furniture at her. But she would go get sewn up and go right back. I could understand that to a point. But like I told her, she and Jesse didn't have kids, thank God, so she just needed to leave. I said, "Now you know what I went through but he only beat me with his fists." She didn't stay too long. After that, she'd finally had enough.

The next several court dates would be over my children, mainly Brennon, as his criminal life began and with the strong addiction of drugs. Thanks to Jesse, Brennon had the attitude he could do whatever he wanted and not be held accountable. Or so he thought. He really got into drugs, robbing to get them and hurting people along the way.

The Lasting Effects

Brennon came to live with me at one point, but after seeing he would have rules, a curfew, and drugs were totally out of the question. I would do random drug tests. He decided to go back to Dad's where he had no rules, could come and go as he pleased. Hell, at a young age, they could drink, do drugs, and even have their eleven-year-old girlfriends move in. But they would have to deal with Jesse always accusing them of sleeping with his women. Jesse would beat women in front of them. I heard this from some of the women he beat and my boys. The kids didn't want rules, and they never had any with Jesse. So Brennon would rob elderly women of prescription drugs and money to get his drugs. He would get in trouble in school, beat up his teacher, and put him in the hospital. He would then be banned from all public schools and sent to a minimal lockup facility until he completed his GED. I thought that would be a lesson learned spending over a year locked up and on lockdown. But sadly, it wasn't.

Brennon would go on stealing, breaking in houses, and abusing elderly people. He took an elderly woman's money, prescription drugs, her credit card and car. Chased by some man, he ends up hitting him with the car and getting away. Brennon would be sent off again. This time in a more secure facility. RPF is what it was called. But even after spending almost two years in there, he did not learn or just didn't care. Every time he got out, Jesse would hand him a pill and get him back on the drugs. And he only done it to help himself. So Brennon would get drugs for him. He didn't care about my son. He was only thinking of himself. Jesse never even wrote Brennon. He never visited him, which I was happy about. I hoped Brennon would straighten up being away from Jesse and not talking to him for a while. Jesse is his poison. Brennon would end up spending all of his teenage years and young adult years behind bars. The judges got tired of seeing him and sent him to prison. He would end up serving his whole sentence due to his anger and attitude, like his dad. I did nothing wrong. Everyone owes me.

He was finally released from prison in 2019, at age twenty-six. It was so sad. It hurt me to have one of my children sent to prison but hurt me more to have one abuse use and hurt people. My son was on a road that would leave him dead or cause him to kill someone. He was hurting so many people, and he had stolen from me for the last time! He had warrants out for his arrest, and the more I heard of what he was doing, the madder I got. Then I feared for his life. He was ripping off drug dealers. After, he'd conned me out of money, or stole it, because he lied. I had given all the kids gift cards for Christmas. Brennon said since it was for Walmart, he couldn't use it, being banned and having a restraining order in place that he not go back to any Walmart store. So I gave him money. He gave me an already used gift card. So I told the police where he was. It was the hardest thing I ever had to do, but he needed a wake-up call, or he would end up dead. I never dreamed he would be sent to prison, but I didn't know all the charges against him. Stealing is wrong. Hurting people is wrong. I do not like a thief. You do not take things that don't belong to you. You do not take from people who have worked hard to get what they might have. You do not hurt people!

Satan Does a Number on My Children

Brennon's anger and attitude got him kicked out of three different prisons. He stayed in trouble in prison. He got time added to his sentence as well. He ended up spending six years in prison when he could have gotten out in eighteen months. He now admits he needed that to wake him up. He is doing good today. He has a baby on the way, a house, cars, good girlfriend, kids, and a good job. But he still has many issues—anger, trust, patience—and he thinks everyone is out to get him. But we have started working on our relationship. And I believe he is truly trying. I am proud of him. I am trying to learn to trust him more each day. God willing, he will be okay.

The same judge who treated me so badly gave Jesse his way and more or less said what Jesse had done was okay. It was the same judge who sentenced Brennon the first few times and expelled him from all public schools. As he looked at me in the courtroom, I felt he knew he had done wrong giving custody to Jesse, but it was too late now. Well, Mr. Judge, I hope you are happy now. And after all the times I had been in his court many times after my divorce, and he had seen what kind of person I really am and what a piece of crap Jesse really is, he seemed to have known he made a bad decision back then. Or that's the vibe I got, and the look I got from him. But it's too late now. He can't give me back what he took and helped destroy.

Jesse would try to bully the boys until they got bigger and older. And I think he was kind of scared of Andrew. When Andrew got mad and in his face, Jesse would back off. He would use the boys and play his sympathy card with them to get things. He had them steal for him. If they worked, they had to give him just about all their money. He charged them for living with him. Something I never done. I tried to help them save money to have things, but I guess having no rules at Jesse's was much better. Amos is the only one who graduated high school, and that's because he lived with Marvin and me at the time. The kids always said living with me was like being in prison. I was a workaholic, and it was boring at my house. Well, I guess if you have no rules, you can drink, do drugs, have sex, stay out for days, and come and go as you please. What kid wouldn't want that?

Jesse always told the boys they weren't his. Especially Andrew. He would tell him that he was his uncle Butch's son. I wish I could say none of the kids were his. I hated that for Andrew. Jesse always treated him badly until he got older and bigger. I always feared Andrew would kill Jesse. Or one of the boys would. Andrew is a lot like me. He is kindhearted, emotional and really cares about people. He wouldn't hurt a fly unless he was forced into a situation. I was afraid Jesse would change that in him.

Jesse would always make the kids feel bad if he knew they wanted to move in with me. He would always tell Danielle if she moved in with me, he'd kill himself. I told her I couldn't get that lucky and "your dad loves himself too much he will not kill himself." She believed him for a long time. Even after she moved in with me, it took a while for her to realize he wasn't going to kill himself. But he tried so hard to get her to move back in with him. She was his cook, his maid. She took care of her brothers over the years, not Jesse. She made sure they got up for school, cleaned the house. She didn't get to be a kid.

What Happened to Our Judicial System?

As the kids got older and opened up to me, told me the things that went on in front of them, it made me sick. And all I could think was, *I hope that judge is happy!* If I could have or could sue that creep, I would in a heartbeat, not just for me but for my kids and all women who were done wrong in court by a judge, by our justice system. The judge not only gave Jesse the right legally to continue his abusiveness, but he sentenced my children and me to a longer life of hell. What part of serve and protect is that? Jesse so screwed my children up. I will never forget the day he brought the kids to me. Andrew was crying, and when I asked him what was wrong, he said, "I am a piece of shit. I'm a no-good p—— and a punk."

I said, "No, you are not, honey. You are a wonderful son, a great person, and don't you ever let anyone tell you different, baby." He was hitting himself in the head and kept saying he was no good and a real p——. What kind of dad tells their child that? Lord, it really made my hate for Jesse grow more. And not just Jesse. I really started to hate that judge. Andrew was so much like me and Daniel. He was real sensitive and emotional he got his feelings hurt easily. So Jesse swore he wasn't his, because he took more after me than the rest of the boys. He was lighter-complected than the other kids. Mainly because he couldn't get Andrew to be mean and talk crap to me like he could the other boys, Jesse hated that. He had to be in full control.

Verbal, Mental, Emotional, Psychological, and Physical Abuse Are All Abuse!

Jesse mostly verbally and emotionally abused my children, which is horrible abuse. All my children were deeply affected by Jesse. And still are dealing with many issues. Danielle ended up marrying a guy pretty much like her dad. She had even been convinced by her dad that a women was to support the man, and whatever he said goes. Luckily, that marriage didn't last too long, as I helped her get out of it. It took years for Danielle to really realize what her dad was, who he really is. And she finally has stopped talking to him and going to see him. After the birth of her two children, she seen that Jesse only thought of himself and wanted everything to be about him. That he used her to get things. He'd call her to bring him money or cigarettes, take him places, yet when she brought his grandchildren around, he never tried to interreact with them. My grandson is really afraid of him. My daughter seen he was the same selfish, evil guy she grew up around, and she didn't want her children around it.

I have to be honest, I was so happy to hear that. I don't want my grandchildren around him. She has overcome the odds against her. I am so proud of her. She still has issues to deal with the rest of her life, but she is strong, and she is doing great. When Danielle had my first grandbaby, my grandson, Jesse was at the hospital. I was really nervous, shaking a little. But I wasn't going to let it ruin Danielle's day. Marvin had to work, so I was up there by myself. Her first husband's family was there, and I tried to stay by them. Jesse came into the delivery room. I just sat in the corner, looking down at first. Then after a little bit, Jesse started telling Danielle in detail what she was fixing to go through. I mean talking like, "Your p—— is gonna get this big," as he showed it with his hands. "And they'll cut your p——." That was enough!

I was trembling, my heart was racing, but I said, "That is enough! This is my daughter's day, and I am sick of your vulgar mouth. They have heard enough of it growing up. This is not about Jesse. This is about my daughter and if you can't shut up, you need to leave!"

He stands up and starts crying, "Baby girl, I guess I better go. I'm not going to be talked to like that." He left the room, and I could breathe.

My son-in-law said, "I am proud of you, Mom. Way to go."

I said, "You see how I am shaking, but I hate his mouth and he had no right to talk like that."

I apologized to my daughter. But she said, "No, thank you, Mom. I wanted him to leave but didn't want to hurt his feelings." But it felt so good to stand up to him. Jesse is so ignorant and just so sick and selfish.

My boys are really having a hard time coping with life. Ray and Andrew can't let the past go. Andrew has even had thoughts of killing his dad. And that was one of my greatest fears for a long time. Andrew has a lot of depression, anxiety, and a few other issues. I just want to take all the pain away. I pray in time, he will get better and better. He has come a long way. Ray has almost overdosed on drugs four times, that I know of. Ray also has many mental issues, it scares me. I am terrified of getting a phone call one day. He is depressed, he hears voices, he's tried suicide several times. He has trust issues, always thinking someone is out to get him. And drug and alcohol addiction doesn't help. I pray every day he will get some help. He is so smart and a joy to be around when he's not on the drugs, alcohol, or having a mental breakdown. It's heartbreaking to me that as his mother, I can't get him professional help because he is over eighteen years.

As a parent or family member, you should be able to request the help from a court to get your child help. Age shouldn't matter. If someone needs help with addiction or whatever it may be, help them. That could stop a lot of crime. But that's just my opinion. Jesse was so horrible to Andrew for years. Telling him he wasn't his father but since he raised him, he was. He has my third grandchild, and he has one the way. He is a good dad to my grandson. My grandson loves his daddy. When he was younger, nobody could hold him if Andrew was around. I just want to take all of his pain away and help him forget the past. Well, put it way back in his mind and not think about it as much.

Jesse told him so many times he was worthless, a big p—— and a piece of s——. I hate him for that. I tell Andrew all the time he is somebody, he is special, and he is good. I wish I could tell them that Jesse wasn't their father, but I can't. I pray in more time, it will get easier for my kids. I hate to say it, but the best thing for them is to stay away from Jesse. Jesse still tries to play that sympathy card to get things from my kids. He still says he may not be their dad but he raised them and took care of them, so he is. What an idiot!

My kids never got one penny of the money I'd send or any of the child support. Danielle and Brennon never got anything from their disability checks. If they needed toothpaste, soap, toothbrush, shampoo, or toilet paper, Jesse had them call me. He had my kids steal clothes and things they needed for school. But once they were old enough to work, Jesse made them give him most of their check for living with him. For Father's Day, they would do drugs with him. Shoot up drugs. Some freaking father! My other boys have great issues as well. But Ray and Amos are really addicted to drugs and alcohol, and abuse women. Ray has tried to kill himself several times. He died on my daughter's floor. She brought him back, and he spent a few days in ICU. He needs help. I have tried so many times to get a judge to commit him in a secure facility, but as always, the judge would say, "That's not why were are here." Ray has had many court dates, and the ones I went to, or knew about, I begged the judge, but no help from our court system once again. That's our wonderful court system! Amos has a lot of issues as well. Being the oldest, he has seen and remembered a lot more than the other kids. Jesse was always accusing him of sleeping with his girlfriends and his second wife. Amos has had an addiction to drugs and alcohol for years. And he was arrested for hitting his girlfriend, which hurt me. He also has trust issues and thinks everyone is out to get him. Depression and anxiety too. I know Amos and Ray have bipolar depression, anger issues, drug addiction, among many other issues.

It really hurts me to hear someone say they are hopeless, there's no hope for them, it's too late. It's never too late! My children can still overcome this. They have come a long way. We should never say there's no hope for someone. They are human, they are people, my babies, and I will never give up on my children. No child should be thrown to the wolves and be forgotten. The court system is to blame for not protecting my children and myself. No matter how old they get, they will always be my babies, and I will always worry about them. I will always love my children dearly. I will always be there for them and try to help them get above this.

Jesse's family disowned him, for the most part. I seen JR one day at the store. He asked how I was doing. He told me how he stopped having anything to do with Jesse after he had seen how he was with the kids. He also said he couldn't stand to be around some of my boys, his nephews; they acted too much like Jesse. News flash: Jesse was the same, if not worse, back when I was stuck with him. They watched him beat me, how he treated me and was teaching my children his evil ways. And yet they didn't bother to help me or my kids then. They all know how I was mistreated by the court, how I was degraded and treated badly by the judge, and not one person offered to help me and stand up to Jesse. And I guess they never have. They just stopped coming around and having anything to do with him. I never understood why no one would stand up to him. And why the police and court system didn't even want to mess with him, and that's why he got away with so much. Butch and Red, both of Jesse's uncles, told me that before they died to get away from him, I deserved much better and he didn't deserve me. Uncle Red told me to hit him in the head with an iron skillet before he died.

We Must Change Our Court System

What I have learned and seen over the years is it's not innocent until proven guilty. It is guilty until proven innocent. And the judge is the judge, jury, and executioner. There are as many crooked and filthy judges as there are cops. And there are a lot of good ones as well. But just because someone cannot afford an attorney, or one party is the first to file with the court, they are automatically guilty in the judge's eyes. So many women have lost custody of their children just because they couldn't afford an attorney. Or their husband filed first. Or a crooked judge who just didn't like women. It does happen! I have met many women who went through the same unjustly court hearing. So many women who are abused, beaten for years, are terrified and afraid to talk and speak up. They are alone and scared, and like in my case, they weren't allowed to speak in court. And that needs to change! It shouldn't matter what the circumstances are, both parties should be able to speak in court. It doesn't take a lawyer to tell the judge you were beaten and controlled by this person.

But it's like a woman has to pay the rest of her life for being with an abusive man, like she should be punished. Having a life of abuse and fear is not by choice. No woman asks to be beaten and controlled. Or to live in pure fear. Pure hell. A mother should never lose her children unless she is proven unfit. There are so many women in prison today just because they lived in fear and had no control over their life and their abuser abused their children. They actually get more time than the one who done the acts. Now what part of that is right? When you are in an abusive relationship, you do not have any control of your life. You are told when to speak, when to move, what to say, how to say it, when to look up, when to get up, when to go to bed, when to eat, bathe, sleep, and how you are to feel. You're afraid to go to sleep at night. And a judge gives women more time than their abuser. A judge takes her children and gives them to the abuser. There is no justice left in our world.

How many times have cops gotten away with a crime? Or a judge, or a lawyer? Because it does happen. They are not all bad, but believe me, there are many who are crooked. We need to have housing, safe housing, for abused women and their children. A place they know they can go until they can get their life straight and on track. Where they can get help with attorney fees and help to get through the court. Where they can feel safe! Not just get them away from the situation and then turn them out on their own. These women need to know they will have the help they need for a long time. All the resources they will need. It takes years and years to get past abuse and be able to cope. And sadly for some women, they aren't ever able to cope.

I strongly believe the court system—the judge, prosecutors, and attorneys—needs to be evaluated and watched in the court room every few months. Along with the law enforcement officers. Something has to be done to see that Americans get treated properly and justly. Innocent until proven guilty. Freedom of speech. Where's our constitutional rights? Our justice system desperately needs improvement. I have talked to so many women who have been treated unjustly by the court, the judge, who had their children taken also. Who weren't allowed to tell their story in court. Who were degraded by the judge. These women were also once married to Satan. This cycle has to end!

This was not at all easy to write. Just thinking about that part of my life, a part I tried so hard to forget, triggered so many painful memories. I'd catch myself having a panic/anxiety attack. But I do feel it needed to be told. I really pray it will help someone. If I can help one woman by telling my story, it was so worth it. If it helps my children somehow heal, it is so greatly worth it. Sometimes we have to face our pain again in order to move on and heal. But we must be strong enough to move on, to move forward. I feel if my children can read my story, it will be more effective than me just telling them. It's still not easy to talk about.

About five years ago, I wrote a letter to Jesse telling him I forgive him. I will never forget what he'd done to me, but in order for healing, I had to forgive. Now with that said, I don't forgive him for what he's done to my children. I asked Danielle to take the letter to Jesse. For one, I wanted her to read it. And I wanted her to see his reaction. She told me he got so irate after reading it, and she knew everything I had said was the truth, because she knows how Jesse reacts to the truth. I told him I forgave him and I thought it was time he tell my children the truth. Of course, I truly knew that was never going to happen. It's all about Jesse, and he can only be the victim. But it did show Danielle some truth. Even though I truly know it wasn't my fault, and I did not deserve to be treated like that, I still have had some guilt over the years. Maybe for not being stronger, for not doing more to get my kids, and for what he done to my kids. I have tried for years to help them move on and heal, but they have to be the ones to do it. All I can do now is support them, love them, and try to guide them. And after all this time, I am done! I am tired of feeling guilty and replaying over and over in my mind the what-ifs. I still have a lot of healing myself. I will not be guilted into doing or giving any more.

I love my children with all my heart and soul. I pray for them daily. I pray God will show them the light and the way to a normal and happy life. A way to finally heal. I will not apologize anymore for what was out of my control. I was a victim. There are many things that I went through, many things Jesse done to me that I did not put in my story, and those are things that will stay between me and the good Lord. And there are many things I can't remember and don't want to remember. I want to ask my readers to please keep myself and my children in your prayers. Please pray for all abused women and children. And if you ever suspect someone is being abused, please pay attention, and if you can, please help them. Just remember they are alone and so very scared. Listen to them and tell them you believe them. Assure them it is not their fault. They do NOT deserve to be treated this way. Offer them help. You may just save a life.

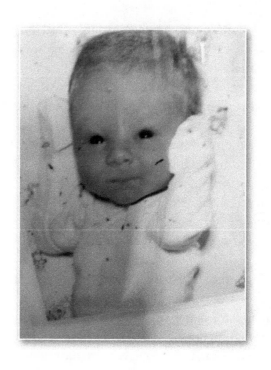

In Loving Memory of My Beautiful Son
My Daniel Lee

I lost my Beautiful Little Angel, almost thirty years ago.
My Heart hurts like the day he left, for time it does not know.

So Beautiful, Sweet and Precious. You were Momma's baby Boy.
The day I gave birth to you, it filled my Heart with Joy.

In a split second, just a blink of an eye, I will never forget that pain.
A part of me died that day, A part I can never regain.

Every year on your birthday, the pain seems more and more.
I didn't get much time with you, You died when you were four.

My Sweet Precious Baby, the day you left, something died in me.
The most Beautiful Little Boy I ever did see. The most Wonderful,
Little Angel, my Son, Daniel Lee.

All I have left are Memories to hold dear to my Heart, A Mother
never gets over losing her Child, it will rip her world apart.

Holding on to Faith and by God's Loving Grace, we'll be together
in Heaven one Day and I can touch your Precious Face.

Until the day I can Hold you again, when life on earth is through.
I Just want you to know how much you are missed, and
how much Mommy loves you.

Tamara Daily
2020

About the Author

About Tamara, well, she is her worst critic. Growing up, she had a dream to be a singer. She loved to sing and loved the times in the car with her mom, listening to her sing. She's always wanted to be like her mom. Her mom is the sweetest, kindest, most loving and caring person she knows. She is far from selfish, and she will do anything for anyone. And her caring got her many beatings. It still breaks Tamara's heart that anyone could be so cruel to her mother and hit her. Like her mother, she always wanted to help people. But when you are with an evil, selfish person, that is not allowed. If she was nice to people, mainly men, she wanted to sleep with them is the way Jesse thought. And it caused a lot of her beatings, just for smiling at someone. She does feel she is a lot like her mom. Her mom inspired her to be like her. Although there is only one of her mom. Tamara is a strong woman, determined, and she cares about people. Jesse may have stolen her dreams, but he could not steal her heart. Now her passion is supporting abused women. She will not stop until she accomplishes the things she feels she needs to get these women. She prays her story will help these women and let them know someone does care. She prays her story will touch Americans enough to want to support these women.

CPSIA information can be obtained
at www.ICGtesting.com
Printed in the USA
BVHW080559300321
603653BV00005B/1003